A SKELETON *in a* DRAWER

A Skeleton
in a Drawer

An Adoption Memoir

MARGARET ALTAZIN

Charleston, SC
www.PalmettoPublishing.com

A Skeleton in a Drawer
Copyright © 2022 by Margaret Altazin

First Edition

Hardcover ISBN: 978-1-68515-763-0
Paperback ISBN: 978-1-68515-764-7
eBook ISBN: 978-1-68515-765-4

For my sister, Diane, who was the inspiration and focus of my memoir. Sadly, she passed away from Alzheimer's Disease before I could complete my work.

CHAPTER 1

Confronting the Discovery

1958

I stuffed my hands in the pockets of my capri pants so Mama wouldn't notice how badly they were shaking, and using my shoulder, I pushed open the squeaky, swinging door that led into our kitchen. Suddenly, the eerie sound of the door closing behind me sent chills up and down my spine. The secret I had discovered in 1953 when I was ten years old, terrified me to reveal it to Mama, but the occurrence of so many traumatic events since then had finally convinced me I had no choice. Taking a deep breath, my voice trembling, I asked, "Mama, would you mind going into the living room with me? I need to talk to you about something especially important."

As she turned to look at me, I knew she could see the fear and dread written on my face. Immediately turning off the water faucet, she dried her hands on her apron and asked, "What's wrong, Baby? You look like you've seen a ghost!" *No, not a ghost, Mama, but I did find a scary skeleton in a drawer,* I thought to myself. Not wanting to have this discussion while standing in the kitchen, I repeated my request to go with me into the room in our house where we held all serious family discussions.

"Okay, let's go," she said, as she pushed the door open for me and followed me into the living room. When I heard the squeaky door shutting behind her, I found myself saying a silent prayer that the upcoming conversation would finally shut my mind's door on the nightmare I had been carrying around.

Once in the living room, Mama sat in her favorite maroon platform rocker, and I sat, legs crisscrossed, facing her on our sectional sofa.

Sitting quietly in those positions for what seemed an eternity, she finally broke the silence. "Margaret, you're scaring me. You know there is nothing in the world you can't talk to me about." Summoning all the strength and courage I could muster, I took a deep breath, and blurted out the question that had been haunting me for five years. "Mama, am I adopted?"

As soon as the words were out of my mouth, I felt such a physical and emotional release, as if someone lifted a heavy weight from my shoulders. Anxiously awaiting an answer, I searched her face for a reaction, but all I saw was her eyes well up with tears. She then raised her hands to cover her face, and her shoulders started shaking as she sat silently crying.

I was aware my question was the last thing she would ever have expected me to ask her and knowing it must have come as a terrible shock, I tried my best to sit patiently and allow her all the time she needed to answer my shocking question. While waiting, my thoughts drifted back to that fateful day five years ago when that skeleton changed my life forever.

CHAPTER 2

Discovering the Skeleton

1955

It was a dreary, late March afternoon, which started differently than the usual after-school days, because my best friend, Bonnye, had not walked home from school with me. Sister Althea, our English teacher who was a handwriting fanatic, could not abide Bonne's "scribbling," as she called it, so she had been detained after school to practice her cursive penmanship. Bonnye and I had been best friends since first grade and were now in seventh grade at St. Anthony Middle School. Since we lived just two blocks away from each other in Northdale, a middle-class neighborhood in Baton Rouge, Louisiana, and our school was within a reasonable walking-distance of our houses, we often walked home together in the afternoons, weather allowing.

I had always dreamed of having a sibling, not only because I was lonely when my best friend was not around, but because I felt somehow deprived, being the only student in our class of thirty-nine at school who did not have one. Bonnye, on the other hand, had an older sister named Carole, with whom she shared a bedroom in their two-bedroom house. Insisting I was lucky to be an only child, she often told me stories about Carole's bossiness, such as ordering

Bonnye out of "her" bedroom, as she called it, when she was on the telephone, doing homework, or having one of her friends over to visit. Staying at my house provided a break from her sister, so she came over most afternoons after school, and spent weekends with me, if her mother didn't have other plans for her.

I lived with my mother, Lucy, who I called "Mama," my father, Arthur, whom I had called "Honey" since I first learned to talk, and my ancient, orange-colored long-haired cat named Rhubarb. Both my parents worked, Mama as a beautician and Honey as a police officer, so most days I was alone after school. Since they thought of Bonnye as a second daughter, Mama and Honey always welcomed her to our house, plus they were grateful to have someone keep me company in the afternoons. If she was still at our house when Mama arrived home from work, she included Bonnye in our supper plans, if she called her mother for permission.

Having been born and raised on a farm in Duplessis, a French-influenced town in rural south Louisiana, Mama always referred to our evening meal as supper, which comes from the French word "souper" meaning the last meal of the day. Even while holding down a full-time job, Mama kept up her ancestors' tradition of cooking a full-course country meal every night.

After supper, Bonnye and I always cleared the half of our formal dining room table, which Mama kept covered with an everyday tablecloth on which we ate our informal meals. She stacked the other half of this beautiful table with piles of "junk," as I called it. After we helped Mama dry and put away the dishes, I walked Bonnye halfway back to her house, if she wasn't spending the night. The walk to her house only took minutes since we took shortcuts through our neighbors' yards. When we reached our destination, our parting ritual was always the same. We hugged, and recited the words of the popular catchphrase, "See you later alligator."

After arriving home alone on this fateful day, I opened the front door with the key my parents kept hidden under one of the flowerpots on the front porch. As I walked into the living room, I turned on our eighteen-inch Zenith black-and-white television set, dialed the channel tuner to ABC, and heard the strains of "Bandstand Boogie" fill the room. Setting my books down on the dining room table, I made my way into the kitchen to fix my favorite snack of a banana, peanut butter, and mayonnaise sandwich. I then retraced my steps to the living room, carrying my sandwich in one hand and a glass of milk in the other. Pausing as I passed through the dining room again, I cringed when I saw the disarrayed condition at the far end of the table. My thoughts were suddenly interrupted, however, by a rumbling in my stomach.

Continuing into the living room, I settled down on the floor in front of the TV and ate my snack, wishing Bonnye were with me. Watching *American Bandstand* together, we couldn't resist taking off our loafers, and in our sock-feet trying out the latest Jitterbug steps to the rock-and-roll music blaring from the television set. Dancing in my living room was especially fun because Honey kept our hardwood floors beautifully polished and buffed, the sweet smell of the paste wax filling our nostrils, and the slippery, open surface area in the room large enough for us to perform our dance moves without bumping into furniture. I turned off the TV when *American Bandstand* was over and sat in the living room, trying to decide what I would do for the rest of the afternoon.

I walked to the kitchen to put my empty glass in the sink and returned to the dining room to pick up my books from the table. I paused for a couple of minutes to admire the beautiful mahogany Duncan Phyfe dining room set, which consisted of a table with six upholstered-seat, lyre-back chairs, a buffet, and a china closet. Sadly, however, Mama had a beautiful ecru-colored, hand-crocheted tablecloth on the table, but kept it folded back on the far end where she stacked her junk: newspapers, junk mail, bills, coupons, green stamp books, and other miscellaneous items. The only exception to this daily eyesore was if Mama and Honey invited company for supper, in which case Mama hid the junk in the hall closet and covered the table with her formal tablecloth.

This chaotic accumulation of worthless stuff, however, reminded me of advice Mama gave me one day when I was younger about the financial struggles she and her family faced while she was growing up. "Margaret, she said, we should always be thriftful and not throw away things just because we think they are worthless at the time. One day we may regretfully wish we had one or more of those items back because we discovered a practical use for them." I tried following her advice as best I could, but I, on the other hand was compulsive about keeping my things at home and at school organized and arranged as neatly as possible.

Staring at one of the chairs, a memory popped into my head of how excited I felt the first time Mama and Honey had allowed me to sit on one of the grownup chairs, with a booster seat added, and eat at the "big" table with them. The soft feeling of the chair seat's satiny material and the fun of tracing the lyre on the back of the chair with my fingers, brought back happy memories.

Hearing Rhubarb meow as he rubbed against my legs returned me to the present. With my books in one arm, I reached down and picked him up, looking back at the table as I headed to my bedroom. An idea suddenly struck me as to how I could spend the rest of the afternoon. I was going to transform the appearance of the dining room table.

After putting Rhubarb on my bed, and my books on my desk, I changed into a pair of comfortable blue capri pants and one of Honey's old shirts, which I tied at my waist. Sitting down on the stool of my dresser I unwound the tight rubber band, holding my ponytail in place, and brushed through my long blonde hair, instantly giving relief to the dull headache I had. Staring at myself in the mirror, I saw my eyes reflecting excitement at the project I was about to undertake. Describing the color of my eyes was difficult. They changed from blue, greenish, gray, or hazel, depending on the color of the blouse or shirt I was wearing. Today, since Honey's shirt was baby blue, with darker blue stripes, blue eyes stared back at me,

Getting up from my stool, I noticed Rhubarb stretched out on my bookshelf among the basketball, volleyball, bowling, and softball trophies I had won over the years. I smiled at the agility he still had at the age of fifteen to conduct this graceful feat without knocking any of my trophies off the shelf. Leaning over, I gave him a kiss on the head and walked back into the dining room, stared at the table, took a deep breath, and dove into my project.

I knew, with Mama being so frugal, I couldn't risk throwing away any of the stuff without having to face her anger, so I started by sorting everything into like-sized stacks: newspapers, junk mail, bills, coupons, church bulletins, green stamp books, and other miscellaneous items. The only things I put aside were a couple of letters from Mama's mother, whom I called Grandma. I carefully placed each separate pile neatly on the seat of the dining room chair opposite Honey's "head-of-the-table seat." Standing back, I inspected my work, and mentally gave myself a pat on the back.

The stacks of stuff on the chair were not even visible since the lovely, hand-made crocheted tablecloth draped beautifully, covering the chair seat completely. Removing the "everyday" tablecloth from the area where we ate our meals, folding it, and placing it on the chair seat as well, I unfolded the crocheted tablecloth and covered the entire table with it. Then, moving Mama's Fostoria compote filled with plastic fruit from the buffet to the center of the table, I stepped back and proudly gazed at the amazing transformation.

Seeing Grandma's letters still laying at the other end of the table, a pleasant memory of our Sunday lunch gatherings at her house in the country came to mind. A houseful of relatives was always there since Mama had six siblings and seven nieces and nephews near my age. My cousins and I loved exploring in the woods, playing "Tarzan" by swinging on the vines of the old oak trees behind her house, building forts, and playing hide-and-seek. I shuddered, remembering the spiderwebs clinging to all the corners in Grandma's outhouse, since spiders terrified me.

Returning to the present, I looked down at the letters in my hand and decided to put them in the center drawer of the china closet because I knew this was where Mama kept her personal papers. When I opened the drawer, the amount of stuff that Mama had crammed inside this small space left me stunned. Deciding to organize this drawer too, I pulled out all the contents to arrange them in order, and noticed one piece of yellowed paper, appearing older than the rest, stuck to the bottom of the drawer.

Of course, my ten-year-old curiosity got the best of me. What harm could a little snooping do? Very carefully unfolding the yellowed document, I found myself looking at my baptismal certificate from St. Agnes Catholic Church in Baton Rouge. I started to refold it and place it back in the drawer, but an eerie sensation overcame me as a voice whispered in my ear, '*Read it, don't put it back.*' I hesitated, curious about what could be so important about my baptismal certificate. I decided to listen to my inner voice and started reading the document. Starting at the top, I scanned down to the bottom and froze in shock!

I found myself staring in horror and confusion at the names the document listed as my parents, as they were not Mama and Honey's names, but two people I had never heard of before. Taking deep breaths to try and stay in control of my emotions, and with shaking hands, I slowly and carefully re-read the entire document. It correctly listed the spelling of my name, as well as the date and place of my birth, Gulfport, Mississippi. I kept staring at the names on the bottom of the page and was unable to make sense of what I was seeing. Re-folding the document, I carefully placed it back on the bottom of the drawer and piled the rest of the papers on top of it, including the new letters from Grandma. The pride I had felt at transforming the disastrous table into a thing of beauty suddenly dissolved into an uglier mess, one which I had no idea how to straighten out.

Dazed by this revelation, I slowly walked to my bedroom, closed the door and stumbled to my bed, and lied down. I felt dizzy from the questions swirling around in my head. *How could this be possible? Did the church make a mistake? Was there another person who shared my name and date of birth? Could the church have accidently switched the parental information? Why was it hidden away in the bottom of the drawer?* There was one frightening question, however, which crept into my thoughts. *Is it possible that Mama and Honey are not my real parents? Could they have adopted me?*

I answered aloud, "That's ridiculous, Margaret! Mama and Honey would surely have told me years ago if they had adopted me."

My mind drifted as I lay on the bed. Random thoughts, pictures and memories started bombarding me, and suddenly, a particular memory from years ago, came to mind. I remembered hearing a conversation between Mama and Honey after he returned home from work one night. "Well, Dear," he said, I'm proud to say I finally caught the male suspect we have been looking for. I always knew he was guilty but was unable to prove it until I discovered the secret his family had been hiding for so long. You know, like the old saying goes, 'Most people have skeletons in their closets which they try to keep hidden, but eventually those secrets have a way of being discovered.'"

Remembering how frightened I was at hearing that story, I asked Honey the next day if people really do keep skeletons in their closets. He chuckled, picked me up, sat me on his lap, and said, "'Baby, I wasn't talking about real skeletons. 'Skeletons in a closet' is just a saying to explain that some people have secrets in their families they don't want anyone else to know about. They keep them hidden, like hiding something in your closet, your diary for example, that you don't want anyone else to find. But let's say someone opened the closet door, saw your diary, read it, and discovered your secret. I'm sure their discovery would have upset you as much as if they had found a real skeleton. Does that make sense to you now?'"

I nodded my head and said, "Honey, I hope I never find a secret in someone's closet, because I don't want to be the one to let a skeleton fall out."

Realizing I had just discovered a skeleton in our family, the skeleton Mama and Honey had hidden wasn't in a closet, but they had tucked it away in a drawer.

Mama interrupted my thoughts when she called out, "Baby, I'm home." I listened to her footsteps as she walked through the living room, but instead of continuing to her bedroom as usual, her footsteps abruptly stopped. "Margaret Ann, what in the world did you do to my table and where is all my stuff that was on it?" At once I knew I was in trouble because Mama only used both of my names when she wasn't happy with me.

Responding angrily, and in a sarcastic tone of voice, I said, "Don't worry, I didn't throw away any of your precious junk, it's all on the seat of the chair at the end of the table we never use." I waited for a reprimand because I knew I had been disrespectful, but instead, I heard her footsteps approaching my bedroom.

She opened my door, stuck her head in, and said, "Don't you ever talk to me in that tone of voice again, young lady!"

Begrudgingly, I apologized. "I'm sorry, I guess I'm grumpy because I have a headache."

"Margaret, I'm sorry you have a headache, but that is no excuse for being disrespectful. I'll bring you aspirin, and then I expect you to come to the supper table with a better attitude and with a smile on your face."

CHAPTER 3
Life-Changing Events

1958

Returning to the present, I sat gazing out the living room window at the clouds and drizzling rain and realized the weather outside reflected my inner mood. I looked over at Mama and she was still sitting there, looking down at her hands, still folded in her lap. Trying patiently to allow her all the time she needed to answer my question, I allowed my thoughts to drift away again and take me down the bumpy road of emotional events that led to today's confrontation.

The day after the devastating discovery of my baptismal certificate, I knew I had to share this experience with someone. Of course, the first person that came to mind was my best friend, Bonnye. I waited impatiently for a sign to tell me when and where I should share his traumatic revelation with her.

A week later, as we were casually walking home from school on a beautiful spring day, listening to the chirping of the birds, smelling the sweet fragrances of the gardenias, freshly cut St. Augustine grass, and admiring the beautiful deep pink azalea bushes, a feeling of peace overcame me. As we crossed the Mulberry Street Canal, and I heard the familiar sound of its' trickling water, splashing against the rocks below the bridge, the peaceful feeling stopped me suddenly, and I realized, this was the perfect place for me to share my shocking news with my best friend.

Bonnye, noticing I had stopped, turned around and walked back to me. "Margaret, is anything wrong?"

As I started scooting down the steep embankment toward the water, I hollered back at her, "Come on, slowpoke! I have a huge secret to share with you."

She quickly scrambled down the hill and sat next to me on our special rocks. Even though our mothers didn't approve of us playing by the canal, we snuck off occasionally to skim rocks across the water, search for crawfish in their little mud houses, or just share juicy gossip from school.

Sitting in silence, all I could hear was the rippling of the water and the pounding of my heart. Bonnye finally broke the silence and said, "A penny for your thoughts." Hearing her use one of our favorite sayings, I couldn't help but smile, her words giving me the courage to begin.

Turning to her, I said, "You have to swear you will never repeat a word of what I'm about to tell you."

She made the sign of an "X" over her heart, raised her right hand, and pledged, "Cross my heart and hope to die."

Taking a deep breath, I asked, "Do you remember Tuesday of last week when you had to stay after school and didn't come home with me?"

"Uh-huh, why?" she asked.

Picking up a rock to skim across the water, I continued, "After watching *American Bandstand*, I couldn't figure out what to do since you weren't there, so I decided to clean off Mama's mess on the dining room table and I found a couple of old letters from Grandma in one of the piles of junk. I decided to put them in the drawer of the china closet where Mama keeps her personal papers. When I opened the drawer, another jumble of papers stuffed in it urged me to clean it out also. Being such a neatnik, I also started straightening it. At the very bottom was a yellowed piece of folded paper which was stuck to the bottom. I couldn't resist seeing what it was, so I carefully removed it, but was disappointed to see it was just my baptismal certificate. I started to put it back when I heard a little voice say, *Read it, Margaret.* So, I did, and you will never believe what I found! My baptismal certificate did not list Mama and Honey as my parents, but two names which I had never heard of before. You know what this means, don't you?" I practically screamed at her.

Bonnye was sitting with her mouth and eyes wide open, and finally she started nodding her head up and down.

I said the scary words aloud, "I'm afraid this means I'm adopted."

We sat in silence, letting the words settle in, and finally, my best friend in the entire world said the only thing she could think of to help me feel better, "Margaret, I'm adopted, too."

Staring deeply into her eyes, I suddenly burst out laughing. "I love you for saying that Bonnye, but I know it is impossible. You look too much like your mother, daddy, and sister."

Her eyes suddenly teared up. Standing, and pulling me up with her, she gave me a big hug and said, "Margaret, even if you are adopted, it doesn't change who you are, and you will always be my best friend in the whole wide world." My laughter turned to tears, and the next thing I knew we were hugging and crying together.

The next Sunday, Mama, Honey, and I set off on our usual thirty-mile trip to Grandma's house in the "country," as we called it, for our family get-together. When we pulled into her huge front yard filled with pecan trees, and cows grazing in the pastures around the house, I noticed my uncles sitting on the front porch in their rocking chairs. Suddenly, I felt a peculiar sense of dread. Getting out of the car, I managed to avoid the cackling chickens strutting free-range around Grandma's yard and helped Mama remove two pecan pies and a bowl of banana pudding from the back seat of our car. We carried the desserts into the house while Honey closed the gate behind us to keep the cows in the yard. Then he made his way to a rocker on the front porch to join in the men's conversations.

When Mama and I entered Grandma's house, scrumptious aromas from the kitchen welcomed us. At once I recognized one of them as being her famous pot roast stewing in her big, black cast-iron pot on one burner of her gas stove and I knew another mouth-watering smell was that of her homemade biscuits baking in the oven. Standing behind her, I kissed her cheek, and in awe, I admired her skill in spooning up batches of homemade crackling from the black cast-iron skillet, which rested on another burner of the stove, onto a large platter. Suddenly the same eerie feeling I had when we drove into her yard overcame me again, and a frightening thought occurred to me. This woman, whom I have loved all my life, would not be my biological grandmother if Mama and Honey had adopted me, and I wouldn't inherit her phenomenal cooking skills. With tears starting to fill my eyes, I excused myself and hurried out the screened kitchen door to join my cousins in the woods behind the house.

A game of hide-and-seek was already underway, so I had to wait until everyone was "found," and since I was the newest arrival, I was appointed "It" for the next game. Even though I was enjoying our game and the company of my cousins, I still had trouble shaking the troubling thoughts and feelings that struck me when we arrived. Aunt Nell interrupted our game about an hour later, standing on the back porch, yelling at us to wash up at the pump outside the house by the cistern before we set foot in the house for our meal.

As soon as Aunt Nell inspected our hands, to be sure they were clean, she allowed us to enter the house and sit down at the table in our usual places. Bowing our heads, we listened to Uncle Crip as he said the blessing before our meal. Instead of bowing my head, though, I found myself studying the people seated around me, who I feared might not be my flesh-and-blood relatives if Mama and Honey had indeed adopted me. Questions kept swirling around in my head such as: *Do they know the truth? Have they been keeping this secret from me also? Do they love me as much as my other cousins who are their biological children?* I couldn't shake the feeling that I was just an outsider sitting among a group of strangers.

Two weeks after surviving that emotional day at Grandma's, my cousin, Becky, whose parents, Aunt Myrtle, and Uncle Neal, were related to me on Honey's side of the family, invited me to spend the weekend at her house. Becky and I had always been close friends, not just because we were the same age, but also because we played sports together, went to CYO dances together, and had slumber parties at each other's house. When Aunt Myrtle called us, along with Becky's three brothers and one sister, to the table for supper the first night I was there, I again found myself having the same uncomfortable feeling of self-doubt I had felt at Grandma's house, wondering again if these people were my actual flesh-and-blood relatives.

Those two emotional events, although I somehow survived them, left me with added anxiety, new doubts, and fears. Weeks later I again turned to Bonnye to share the uncomfortable new feelings. Having no luck in begging me to tell Mama and Honey about my discovery, Bonnye tried her best to understand why it was so hard for me to do that. Having the heart-to-heart talk with her, however, calmed me, and helped me find the extra courage and strength I needed to keep playing the pretend game of "Everything is Normal" with Mama and Honey.

CHAPTER 4

A Painful School Assignment

I continued to hide my feelings from Mama and Honey for another year. Besides focusing on school and my friends, I kept my mind and body busy by playing softball, basketball, volleyball, swimming, dancing, and bowling in a league.

When I entered tenth grade in the fall, however, determined that I had put the skeleton out of my mind forever, a simple school assignment triggered the demon to start creeping back out of the drawer, and the same insecure feelings flooded over me again.

During the first semester of school, our social studies teacher, Sister Walter, assigned the class a project which involved constructing a family tree and charting our ancestors' names on it. She offered bonus points if we researched genealogy records and discovered previously unknown relatives. Sitting in the classroom in total shock, I asked myself, "*Seriously, you want us to do what? I have no idea of my identity, and you want me to give you information I do not have?* I envisioned the skeleton inching its way out of that drawer, waving at me, and saying, 'Hey, remember me? I'm still here! You can't bury me!'"

When I walked home with Bonnye after school that day, she knew how upset I was about the assignment and begged me,

"Margaret, please tell Mama and Honey about your discovery. This situation is causing you too much stress. It's not healthy."

I knew she was right, but I couldn't explain why something seemed to be holding me back. Arriving at home, we followed our usual after-school routine and then started on our homework. I knew I would be unable to begin the family tree assignment until I worked up the courage to talk to Mama.

The next afternoon, I decided I couldn't put it off any longer. So, while Bonnye was doing her homework in my bedroom, I walked into the kitchen where Mama was preparing supper. I tried my best to keep the frustration out of my voice when I asked, "Guess what Sister Walter assigned us?"

Mama put down the spoon she was stirring the gumbo with, turned to look at me and said, "Baby, I have no idea."

"Well, of all the ridiculous things she could have assigned, she decided to have us construct a family tree and record our ancestors' names on it. She even offered to give us bonus points if we researched genealogy records and discovered previously unknown relatives. I'm afraid I am going to have to ask you to help me with this, since I'm not certain of the names of our ancestors."

Thinking to myself that this would be a perfect time for Mama to tell me that she and Honey had adopted me, I watched closely for a sign she might be ready to tell me the truth. She seemed uneasy, and as she turned again to face the pot simmering on the stove, she was fiddling around with something on the kitchen counter. When she turned and faced me, I held my breath. She said, "Okay, let's go sit down at the dining room table, and I'll give you the names of your grandparents, and great-grandparents I'm aware of on each side of our family, and you can write them down." Disappointed, I joined her at the table after getting a tablet and a pencil from the desk in my bedroom.

After I sat down, Mama started by saying, "Baby, the ancestors on both sides of our family are of Cajun, French, Native American, or of French-Canadian origin. I will start by giving you the names of your grandmothers and grandfathers. Are you ready? I know I'll have to spell the Cajun names for you."

After I nodded yes, she told me each name, as well as spelling the more unusual ones. As I was writing down the information she gave me, I doubted these were really my blood ancestors. Mama then added, "If you'd like help in tracing their ancestry further back, I would be happy to take you to the library and show you how to go about doing that. I helped a friend of mine years ago, who was searching for a long-lost relative, so I know a little about checking census records."

Thinking about her offer, I said, "Thanks. That would be helpful, Mama," while thinking to myself, *I may as well try to get bonus points for this project, because I'm afraid, I'm not learning the truth about my ancestry.*

The next Saturday, Mama got off work early, so she offered to take me to the downtown library, explaining on our way how they stored census records on microfiche in the basement of the building. She said we could use these records to trace earlier generations of our families.

When we arrived, we walked down a flight of stairs to the basement, where an unpleasant, musty odor, overcame me. After hours of searching through the old records, we finally found a previously unknown ancestor on Honey's side of the family, and I had to admit it was exciting to make that discovery. We didn't have any luck, however, researching Mama's families. I could hear disappointment in her voice when she said, "I'm sure the Census Bureau had difficulty gathering ancestral information on my family because they were from very small rural towns in remote areas where census information was rarely taken."

The information Mama gave me, along with the new discovery we found in the library, however, enabled me to create an impressive family tree. The following Monday, I walked to Sister Walter's desk when she called my name and handed her my completed assignment.

Looking it over she said, "Good job, Margaret! You are fortunate to have this much information on your ancestors." As I returned to my desk and sat down, I suddenly felt guilty, wondering if I had committed a sin by turning in information that was not factual.

After this, it became even more difficult to keep my anger, confusion, and anxiety hidden from Mama and Honey, but I still couldn't find the inner strength I needed to confront them with my discovery.

CHAPTER 5

Shocking Revelation

One day, out of the clear blue, Honey sat me down and said, "Baby, I have important news to share with you. I have decided to take an early retirement from the police department, and Mama and I are going to open our own business."

In absolute shock, I responded, "You're kidding, right?" Honey shook his head *no*, but before he could say anything else, I blurted out, "What kind of business, and how in the world were you able to convince Mama to quit her job and join you in starting a business?" Knowing how frugal Mama was, I couldn't imagine her agreeing to this plan. She had always been the one in charge of their financial matters, watching over each penny like a mother hen guarding her chicks. Honey, on the other hand, had always been a dreamer and spender, wishing for the finer things in life, and envisioned self-employment as a means of achieving that goal.

He replied, "No Baby, I'm not kidding, and yes, I did have a tough time convincing Mama. After pondering on my proposal and saying rosaries and novenas for nine days, though, she finally decided this just might provide the extra income we would need to comfortably pay for your college and still leave us with a nice nest egg for our retirement. One of my trusted friends told me that owning an automated car wash businesses can be quite lucrative, so Mama and I have been searching for one we could afford to buy. We finally found one, but the only problem is the location. It is in Kenner, near New Orleans, which is about two hours away from here."

Still reeling from his news, I hesitantly asked, "Does that mean we'll have to move?" Holding my breath as I waited for his answer, he replied.

"No, we're not moving, Baby. Mama and I want you to be able to finish high school here in Baton Rouge with your friends."

Finally exhaling, I said, "Thank goodness. I don't think I would be able to deal with having to move."

Honey continued, "But, I'm afraid there will have to be changes made here at home because we don't want you staying alone when we are gone. We'll have to leave early in the morning and will not be returning home until late in the evening. Luckily, Mama was able to find a nice, retired lady who is willing to come in the mornings and make sure you are awake, fix your breakfast, make your lunch, and get you off to school. She'll return in the afternoons to fix your supper and stay with you until we return home."

Having trouble processing this shocking news, I snapped, "Are you serious? You and Mama are going to hire a babysitter to take care of me?" Storming out of the room, I yelled, "I am fifteen years old! I'm not a baby."

Leaving me he alone in my room long enough to cool down, he quietly walked in later and said, "Margaret, please try to understand that we love you so much and we would be worried knowing you were here alone, fending for yourself every morning and afternoon. We are hoping this arrangement will only be temporary, because we plan to hire another employee as soon as we get the business up and running, which would then allow Mama to stay home."

Calming down at hearing this additional information, I said, "I'm not happy with the arrangement, Honey, but I'll try my best to deal with it, especially since it will only be temporary."

One afternoon a couple of weeks later, I came home from school to find this older lady in the living room with Mama. I'm not sure what I thought a teenager's babysitter would look like, but believe me, this lady did not fit any preconceived picture I might have had. The person I was looking at was a tall, slender lady, dressed very matronly in a stiffly ironed white blouse, plaid skirt, and brown laced-up saddle shoes. She wore her mostly gray hair pulled back into a severe bun at the nape of her neck, and she allowed her eyeglasses to hang on a chain around her neck when she wasn't using them.

Reaching out her hand to me by way of introduction, she said very quietly, "So nice to meet you, Margaret. My name is Edith Broussard, but I would prefer your calling me Ms. Edith."

Remembering my manners, which Mama had strictly taught me as I was growing up, I replied, "Nice meeting you, too, Ms. Edith." After awkward exchanges, I excused myself and went to my room. *Surely, she will be more friendly once we get to know each other,* I thought to myself as I picked up the phone to call Bonnye and give her a report on my babysitter

CHAPTER 6

The Straw That Broke the Camel's Back

As the days settled into a routine, I kept waiting and hoping to see Ms. Edith's rigid, military-like demeanor transform itself into a pleasant, smiling human being, but sadly, it never happened. Constantly hovering over me like a drill sergeant, she barked out commands such as, "Margaret, eat all your breakfast," "Margaret, pick up your things," "Margaret, turn your music down." "Margaret, did you do your homework?" "Margaret, it's time for you to go to bed." I was miserable, forced to live under those conditions for six months, until one day I had an accident at school.

My class was playing basketball on a concrete court during PE when I tripped and fell out of bounds. Unfortunately, I landed on a pile of boards stacked up against one of the classroom buildings on the side of the court, and one of the boards had a nail protruding through it. My PE teacher, Ms. Stagner, called our school nurse, Ms. Cagney, as my leg was bleeding profusely. She performed first aid and informed me it would be necessary for a medical doctor to look at my leg, as it would need stitches. With Mama and Honey's jobs now being out of town, the school secretary called Ms. Edith since Mama had listed her as the emergency contact on my school records.

She explained the situation and told Ms. Edith to meet me and Ms. Cagney at the Baton Rouge General Hospital Emergency Room.

Arriving at the hospital, an ER nurse met me and Ms. Cagney, helped me into a wheelchair, and pushed me to a curtained cubicle. After sliding the curtain back in place, the nurse helped me into the bed and checked my leg. After she had finished cleaning the wound, she picked up a clipboard and pen from the bedside table, sat down on a chair near me and said, "The doctor will be here shortly to look at your leg, Margaret, so while we are waiting for him, I need to gather background information. First, I need you to describe the accident."

Just as I started describing what happened, Ms. Edith pulled back the curtain and said, "Margaret, are you OK? I was so worried when the school called. I telephoned your mother and father, and they made me promise to call them as soon as I found out how you are."

Assuring her I was fine I said, "Please call them now and let them know I'm okay, so they won't worry." I'm sure the worst-case scenario is that the doctor may have to put in stitches." She agreed, and Ms. Cagney volunteered to go with her.

"Now, Margaret," the ER nurse said, "I'm going to ask you some questions about your medical background and your family's medical history." The pain in my leg suddenly seemed to disappear as her statement threw me into a state of panic. Knowing I could answer questions about my personal medical background, I wondered how I would be able to answer questions about my family's medical history.

Suddenly, I started to hyperventilate, which frightened me even more because I had never experienced that before. The nurse at once rushed over, had me sit up and take deep breaths. As I started to breathe normally again, she asked if I was ready to answer the rest of her questions.

With tears running down my face and still struggling to breathe normally, I said, "I'll try my best." She started asking me if there was a history of various diseases or conditions on either side of my family. Suddenly I felt as if a dormant volcano, which I had kept buried deep in my head for years, started building pressure to the point where I could no longer suppress it. The pent-up pressure finally erupted, and I screamed. "I don't know, I think I'm adopted!"

Dead silence descended on the Emergency Room area around me, but the nurse waited patiently for me to calm down. Slowly regaining my self-control, I looked at her and said, "I'm so sorry for that outburst. I have been carrying this secret fear around for a long time."

She responded very sweetly, "It's okay, dear. I'll just let the doctor know you're not aware of your medical history, but I would like to give you a piece of motherly advice. Please tell your parents about your feelings. Believe me, they would want to know."

I thanked her and said, "I promise to give your suggestion serious thought."

The wound in my leg ended up needing stitches, and the doctor prescribed antibiotics to prevent infection, but the wound in my heart was much deeper and much more painful.

After this incident, I knew the time had finally come for me to pull the skeleton out of that drawer and expose it at last. This decision, however, created troubling questions: *Will I be able to rationally accept the answers my parents give me? If they confirm that they did adopt me, will the truth affect our relationship in any way? Will they have information on my birth family's medical background? If not, and I decide to search for my birth family on my own to obtain this information, will I be able to manage the disappointment if I fail?*

CHAPTER 7

The Truth Revealed

Startled by Mama loudly calling my name, I emerged from my trance-like state to hear her asking me, "Are you okay, Baby? I have been calling your name over and over."

"Yes, Mama, I'm sorry, I guess I just drifted off."

Mama hesitated, drew in a deep breath, and finally gave me the answer to the question I had been waiting so long to hear. "Yes, Margaret, Honey and I did adopt you, but before we continue our conversation, please tell me how you found out."

I said, "Remember that day you came home from work and became upset with me for rearranging the dining room table?" Mama nodded as I continued, "Well, when I found two letters from Grandma in the pile of stuff on the table, I decided to put them in the drawer of the china closet where you keep your personal things. Opening the drawer, I couldn't believe the piles of paper you had stuffed in it, so I also tried to straighten it up. I saw a folded yellowish piece of paper stuck to the bottom, so I took it out to see what it was. When I discovered it was only my baptismal certificate, I thought about putting it back, but my curiosity got the best of me, and I asked myself *What harm could there possibly be in reading it?* I'm sure you can imagine how shocked and confused I was when I saw two other names listed as my parents."

Between sobs, Mama managed to say, "It breaks my heart to know you saw the names of your birth parents before we found the courage to tell you ourselves. I can't imagine the jolt you must have felt when you read their names and discovered the truth. Baby, believe me, I feel such great sorrow and guilt that you learned the truth on your own. Honey and I have been wanting to tell you for years that we adopted you when you were three months old, but the timing just never seemed right. We were also worried that you might not love us as much if you knew we had adopted you."

Sitting in stunned silence, trying to grasp Mama's words, a cascade of new feelings overcame me. Besides hearing the traumatic confirmation of my discovery, I also felt a strange flood of relief at finally knowing the truth. Sadly though, I also felt disappointed at learning Mama and Honey were not my flesh and blood. Sorrow for Mama and Honey also crept into my jumble of feelings, realizing they had been living in a state of confusion and fear that I might not love them as much if I found out they had adopted me. Finally, getting up from the sofa, I walked to the platform rocker where Mama sat. I leaned over and put my arms around her. Standing up, Mama and I hugged and cried together until we were weak. Then we both sat down again to continue our emotional conversation.

"Mama, I want you to know that I love you and Honey so much, and nothing could ever change that."

With tears running down her cheeks, she said, "And Honey and I couldn't love you more, even if I had given birth to you. If you would like to hear the story of how we were lucky enough to adopt you, we'll be happy to share it with you, but I think we should wait until Honey comes back to town tomorrow evening and let us tell you together."

Feeling a sense of peace for the first time in five years, I replied, "I would like that very much, Mama."

CHAPTER 8

Sorting through the Emotions

Feeling emotionally drained after our talk, I kissed Mama on the cheek and said, "I'm going to my room to lie down for a while."

"Baby, are you okay?"

I said, "Yes ma'am. I just feel exhausted."

I couldn't wait to share this revelation with my best friend. Her grandmother was visiting from out of town, however, so her mother insisted she stay home this weekend. I hoped she would at least be able to talk on the phone, so I called her from my bedroom Princess telephone. Lucky for me she answered. I asked her, "Can you talk?"

She said, "Sure, what's wrong? I can tell from your voice something happened. Please share."

"I did it!" I practically yelled into the telephone. "I finally confronted Mama this morning and asked her if they had adopted me. I can't begin to explain the confusing feelings I am dealing with now that she admitted I'm adopted. She asked me to wait until tomorrow when Honey gets home from the car wash so they can tell me the complete story of my adoption together."

Bonnye said, "I'm so proud of you, Bestie, for finding the courage to ask them for the truth. I'm here for you whenever you need me, but I need to hang up right now because my mother is calling me. We'll talk again tomorrow. Love you!"

I responded, "Love you too, BFF, and thanks for the support."

I turned on my AM/FM radio instead of playing my 45 RPM records, so I wouldn't have to get up and restack them after they had all finished playing. I closed the door to my room so Mama couldn't hear my music, because when I left her, she was crocheting and listening to Guy Lombardo's Orchestra on their new stereo in the living room.

Picking up Rhubarb from his favorite perch, I settled down on my bed, listening to the hypnotic purring of my cat and the "Easy Listening" music on the radio station I had selected. My thoughts drifted back to a story Mama told me years ago when I asked her to tell me about her childhood growing up in the country and about how she and Honey met.

"Margaret," she said, "I was born during World War I, and after the war ended our country was suffering economically, and it was difficult for people to make ends meet. As you know, I lived with my mother, father, three brothers and two sisters. Papa worked our farm from sunrise to sunset, plowing with his mule, Bramble, while Mama not only tended to us children, but worked in the garden, and took care of the chickens we raised. When we were old enough to go to school, our transportation was on horseback, as there were no school buses, and the school was too far away for us to walk. Mama and Papa expected us to help with the chores on the farm when we got home from school in the evenings and on weekends. My brothers worked in the fields with Papa, and Aunt Jennie and I helped Mama pick eggs, tend to the garden, and see to the needs of our younger siblings. Tragically, Papa died of a heart attack when he was just thirty-seven years old, and his death left Mama in charge of taking care of the farm. My two older brothers had to drop out of school to help Mama by taking over Papa's field jobs. Your Aunt Jennie and I, being the oldest girls, also had to quit school to help the family.

Our responsibilities were feeding the chickens, gathering the eggs every day, helping in the garden, and taking on more responsibility in caring for our younger brothers and sister. With the entire family pulling together, however, we were able to eke out a decent living.

When I was nineteen years old, Aunt Jennie got married, and Mama encouraged me to leave home and pursue a trade since circumstances had not allowed me the opportunity to finish school. With the money I earned from selling eggs, I had saved enough to take a bus to Baton Rouge, and I rented a room at a boarding house. Luckily, I was able to get a job at Kress' Five and Dime Store, withing walking distance of my room. Shortly after, I enrolled in and completed beauty school, receiving my certification as a licensed beautician.

One night, a friend from work invited me to go to a bash with her at the local VFW Hall. While I was dancing with an acquaintance, someone tagged him to dance with me, and that young man just happened to be Honey. It was love at first sight! We dated until he enlisted in the Navy at the beginning of World War II, and we decided to get married before he was to report for basic training in Gulfport, Mississippi so I would be able to move with him. During the years we lived there, we found ourselves struggling financially due to the negative effects of the Great Depression."

I think the rest of this story will have to wait for another night, Baby. It's time for you to go to sleep.

Thinking back on Mama's story tonight, I realized how profoundly her upbringing had shaped her life. The challenges she and her siblings faced had caused them to be extremely thrifty. And if it were not for Mama continuing to be frugal, proved by hoarding all items she thought may serve a practical use in the future, I would never have found the skeleton in that drawer.

CHAPTER 9

The Day of Reckoning

The morning sun peeking around the curtains into my bedroom awoke me. I rolled over and looked at the clock radio on the headboard of my bookcase bed, and it revealed the time as nine thirty-five a.m. A feeling of anticipation flooded over me, like the feeling you get when waking up on Christmas morning. Trying to clear the cobwebs from my sleepy head, I excitedly remembered the reason for this feeling. I had confronted Mama about my adoption yesterday, and when Honey arrives home from Kenner today, they are going to share the details with me. Glancing at the clock, I realized I needed to rush if I was going to be ready in time to attend Mass at 11:00 a.m. with Mama. We always arrived at church early enough for her to say the rosary before Mass began. Jumping out of bed, I was eager to face this long-awaited day!

After Mass and lunch, the rest of the afternoon seemed to drag by as I waited for Honey to arrive home from work. After trying unsuccessfully to read or take a nap, I finally heard his car pulling up into the driveway. Struggling to be patient, I remained in my room to allow him time to drink the cup of coffee Mama always had ready for him.

After what seemed an eternity, I heard a tap on my door. Mama stuck her head in and said, "Honey and I are ready to talk to you whenever you are, Baby." I put away the book I had been trying to read and followed her into the living room.

As soon as we were all settled in our usual places, Honey started off the conversation. "Margaret, it broke my heart when Mama told me you accidentally found out about your adoption. We have been wanting to tell you for years, but somehow the timing never seemed right, and the longer we waited, the harder it was to find the words. I know you're aware I was a shore patrol officer in the Navy during World War II in Gulfport, Mississippi, where you were born. Since Mama and I were married, I was able to live off-base with her in a little rental house. Shortly after settling in, Mama was lucky enough to find a job as a greeter at the local Markham Hotel. You need to understand, Baby, our country was rationing items, such as food, clothes, gasoline, and other necessities to support the military's needs during the war. All citizens were issued ration books with stamps in them, which we could only use to buy the specific items the government rationed that month, and if we ran out of stamps, we couldn't buy that item again until the next month. It was difficult to make ends meet from month to month, but since Mama was lucky enough to have found a job, we were able to keep our heads above water. Since Mama and your birth mother worked together, Mama knew her better than me, so I'm going to let her finish the story."

I turned my head to look at Mama as she continued Honey's story. "Margaret, I had been working as a greeter at the Markham Hotel when I first met your birth mother, Mary. She went by the name Mayme at work because she preferred it to her given name. She started working at the hotel waiting tables in January of 1943. One day, after selecting my lunch from the cafeteria offerings, I looked around for a place to sit. I spotted an attractive young woman with medium length, curled blondish-brown hair, who was sitting alone at a table. I walked over and asked if she would mind if I joined her.

"She smiled up at me and said, 'Please sit down. I would love company. I've only been living in Gulfport a brief time and haven't made any friends yet.'"

"We had a pleasant lunch together, just chatting about our jobs, the war, and the state of the economy. From that day on, we looked for each other to share our lunches. A couple of months later, she asked me if I would mind meeting her somewhere after work, because she wanted to discuss a personal problem with me. I told her I would be happy to meet her, and I suggested we just walk across the boulevard from the hotel and sit on the seawall since it happened to be a pleasant early spring day.

"Margaret, first let me give you a little background about the seawall. Because of the hurricanes coming in from the Gulf of Mexico, the state built an eight-step concrete seawall along the coastal towns in Mississippi, funded by each county charging an extra gasoline tax. It was a favorite spot of residents and tourists to sit and admire the beauty of the Gulf, listen to the sounds of the seagulls and waves as they crashed onto shore, and watch the dolphins as they played in the water.

"I was the first to arrive at the seawall that afternoon and was sitting on one of the steps when I saw Mayme approaching, waving at me while holding the hand of a little blonde-haired girl, who was dragging a Raggedy Ann doll behind her. I stood up and waved back.

"Hurrying towards me, she apologized for being late, saying she had to pick up her daughter from the babysitter. I told her it wasn't a problem and then asked the name of her beautiful daughter. She told me her name was Diane.

"The three of us settled down on one of the steps and Mayme and I again talked about work, war, and the economy. When Diane moved down a couple of steps to play with her doll, Mayme changed the subject and told me, since I was the only friend she had in Gulfport, she needed advice about a problem she was facing. I told her I would be more than happy to help her if I could. She began by telling me about the circumstances which brought her to Gulfport."

Before Mama could continue with her story, I interrupted. Stunned by the information I had just heard, I exclaimed, "Wait a minute! Are you saying I have a sister? If so, how could y'all have kept something that important from me all these years?"

The tension in the room was so thick it felt as though someone could have cut through it with a knife. Honey finally broke the strained silence and said, "Margaret, Mama and I have felt so guilty for also keeping this secret from you, but there was no way for us to tell you about your sister without telling you about your adoption. And just to be clear, Diane would be your half-sister if she were to still be alive. Let Mama continue and she will give you further details as she continues Mayme's story."

I nodded my head and turned back to Mama. She continued, "I agree with Honey, but let me explain one more dilemma we were facing. Knowing you have always wanted a sibling caused us to worry that you might insist on looking for Diane, and of course in the process, you could find your birth mother as well. We were scared that if this were to happen, you might choose her over us. Baby, there is something else I want you to know about Diane. When we agreed to adopt you, we tried our best to adopt her as well, but Mayme wouldn't allow it."

Silence fell over the room again. Mama and Honey were mourning lost opportunities they had in telling me that they had adopted me, and I was mourning the existence of a half-sister I never knew I had and whom I would never meet.

Mama finally asked, "Baby, do you want me to continue with Mayme's story?"

Nodding my head, I said, "Yes, please. I need to understand why my birth mother gave me away."

CHAPTER 10

Mayme's Dilemma

Mama began by saying, "I'm going to tell you, as accurately as I can remember, what Mayme shared with me. She told me that she graduated from high school in 1939, but I can't for the life of me remember the name of the school or the city. It seems like it may have been either in Ohio or Illinois. Anyway, right after graduation, she met a guy named Charles at a dance one night, and said he was a real dreamboat. He was two years older than her, had his own car, a decent job, and loved dancing. His being a good dancer was important to Mayme because she was an excellent dancer. Honey and I attended a dance at a local club one night, and we invited her to go along with us. Watching her performance on the dance floor, switching from one dance partner to another, provided quite a bit of entertainment,

"Let me get back to the story. While dating Charles, she told me she had heard rumors about his reputation as being quite a lady's man but figured she would be able to change his ways when they settled down and got married. At that time, Mayme was living at her great-grandmother's house with her grandmother, her mother, and her younger brother. They had also heard the rumors about Charles' reputation, didn't approve of him, and unlike Mayme, were convinced he would never change.

"Mayme ignored their warnings, and she and Charles started dating steadily and a couple of months later he asked her to marry him, and of course, she said yes.

"Since Charles had been living with his own family, which was quite large, he didn't have a place of his own where he and Mayme could live. Unable to find an affordable place to rent, Mayme asked her great-grandmother, grandmother, and mother if they would allow her and Charles to move in with them after the wedding. Her great-grandmother was not happy about the arrangement, but finally agreed to consider it after she discussed her expectations of Charles' behavior with him. She told Diane if he agreed to her terms, she would allow them to move into her house.

"The following day, upon returning from work, Mayme and Charles sat down in the living room of her ancestor's house, and in a business-like tone of voice her great-grandmother explained the rules she would expect Charles to follow. First, she would require him to do his share of work around the house, secondly, he would treat the entire household with the utmost respect, and most importantly, he would have to put his rakish behavior behind him. After giving it little thought, he agreed, and Mayme and Charles were married and moved in the next week.

"A couple of months later, Mayme discovered she was going to have a baby. After the initial shock wore off, she and Charles initially became excited about the idea, but just weeks later she told me she noticed he started changing, becoming irritable and difficult to get along with.

One day, her aunt, trying to cheer her up, invited her to go to a movie with her. After finding seats in the theatre, they sat down. Charles, who ironically had been sitting a couple of rows ahead of them happened to turn around and saw Mayme. She noticed him, sitting with his arm around another woman at the same time. Temporarily too shocked to react, she finally started trembling and crying, so her aunt rushed her out of the theater and managed to calm her down once they were outdoors in the fresh air.

"Later that night, when he returned home, she confronted Charles. He profusely apologized and assured her that the woman was his boss's daughter who had come from out of town for a visit, and his boss had asked him to take her to a movie. He swore there was nothing romantic going on between them and promised he would never let anything like that happen again.

"Mayme wanted to believe him so badly that she decided to give him a second chance, mostly because of their soon-to-be-born baby. Their daughter, Diane, was born in September of 1940, but instead of her birth bringing them closer together, Mayme said it drove them further apart. The next week, a friend of Mayme's told her she had seen Charles with another woman at a local bar. Hurt and angry, Mayme confronted him again, but this time she demanded he move out and informed him she was going to file for a divorce as soon as possible.

"After Charles moved out, Mayme took a job waiting tables at a local diner to help her family financially, leaving Diane at home with her family during the day. A couple of months later, a young man, who always asked the host to seat him at one of Mayme's tables, finally found the courage to introduce himself to her as Lonnie. Mayme told me he was polite, intelligent, quite handsome, and easy to talk with. Discovering they had common interests and enjoyed each other's company, they started dating regularly and quickly fell in love. Lonnie told Mayme he wanted to marry her as soon as she was able to get a divorce from Charles and would love nothing more than to raise Diane as his own.

"Unfortunately, Baby, the United States had just become engaged in World War II and the Army drafted Lonnie in 1942. Not long after he arrived at his assigned base in Gulfport Mayme discovered she was expecting another baby, with Lonnie, of course, being the father. Since her family was strong Catholics, who had immigrated from Hungary, they told her they would not allow an unmarried woman, carrying a baby, to remain living under their roof,

"Not sure what to do or where to go, Mayme finally decided to catch a bus to Gulfport and tell Lonnie about the baby in person. She sent him a letter telling him that she wanted to move to Gulfport so they could spend time together before the Army assigned him to a base overseas. Lonnie was excited and was happily waiting for them at the bus station when they arrived in Gulfport. As soon as Mayme and Diane stepped off the bus, Lonnie grabbed them up in a bear hug, picked up their meager luggage, and the three of them walked to a nearby café to have a bite to eat and discuss their living arrangements.

"He explained to Mayme he had found a nice, reasonable boarding house, run by a very responsible older lady, who told him she would be happy to keep Diane during the day for a small fee. She had also given him the names of businesses she heard might be looking for workers. Mayme was excited with the arrangements Lonnie had made, but knew she had to tell him about the baby first.

"The server brought them their sandwiches, and after they finished eating, she told Lonnie the news about the baby she was carrying. He was ecstatic at the prospect of being a father, and of course, suggested they get married right away. Tears running down her cheeks, she told him she had tried to contact Charles, but his mother informed her that he had enlisted in the Navy and was on a ship in Auckland, New Zealand, if I remember correctly. Naturally, Lonnie was disappointed, but he was even more devasted when Mayme told him of her family's reaction to the news about her pregnancy. He promised he would do everything in his power to make their relationship work and support her, Diane, and their baby.

"After leaving the café, the three of them took the city bus to the boarding house Lonnie had rented. It wasn't fancy, but it was clean and provided all their basic needs. An extra benefit was the location. It was in the central part of town, which allowed Mayme to walk anywhere she needed to go, and she prayed she would be able to find a job nearby.

"The next day the lady who ran the boarding house kept Diane while Mayme checked out the list of job openings Lonnie had given her. With Mayme's earlier restaurant experience, she started off applying at various cafes and restaurants and was lucky enough to find a job waiting tables at the Markham Hotel, which happened to be within walking distance from her boarding house.

"Knowing the Army could ship him out at any time, Lonnie and Mayme saw as much of each other as possible. They often spent their time just sitting on the seawall as close to the water as possible, allowing Diane to play in the sand. One day, Mayme said, their conversation turned to choosing a name for their baby. They both decided if it were a boy, they wanted to name him Lonnie Junior, but had more trouble thinking of a girl's name. Lonnie finally asked Mayme if she would be okay with the name Margaret, after one of his favorite relatives. She said she liked the name and thought it would be a sweet thing to do, so she agreed.

"A couple of weeks later, Lonnie received orders that he was to be immediately shipped to New Guinea. Exchanging emotional goodbyes, he promised he would help her financially by sending money each month. Mayme was grateful because she was already struggling to make ends meet, between the expenses of the boarding house rent, groceries, and paying babysitting fees for Diane. She told me it was over a month before she finally received a letter from Lonnie, with money enclosed. The mail service was terribly slow, and by the time the small amount of money arrived, she was already in debt.

"You were born in June of that year, and Mayme, having another mouth to feed and now having to pay childcare for two children, was beginning to panic at the financial situation she found herself in. Honey and I helped her as much as we could, but it still wasn't enough for her to make ends meet. She wrote Lonnie after you were born to give him the happy news of your birth, but she also had to share the sad news about her financial struggles.

"Mayme finally received another letter, with money enclosed, but by that time she was deeper in debt. In the letter, however, Lonnie told Mayme he had written his mother about sending his younger sister, Shirley, who had just graduated from high school to Gulfport to help by keeping the children while Mayme worked, which would at least keep her from having to pay a babysitter. Hoping this solution would be the answer to her prayers, Mayme agreed.

"Shirley arrived in Gulfport by bus a week later. The new arrangement seemed to help for a brief time, until Mayme had to bring Diane to the doctor for tonsilitis. Between the medical bills, and the extra grocery expense of feeding an additional adult, Mayme was still not able to make ends meet. She had no choice but to write Lonnie and explain her predicament. He wrote back and agreed it was best for Shirley to return home and he would somehow try to send her additional funds. He told Mayme his mother would have loved for her and the children to move into her house, but unfortunately there was not enough room for three additional people to live there.

"One day at lunch a couple of weeks later, Mayme asked if I would meet her again on the seawall after work. Of course, I agreed.

"When she arrived, she not only had Diane, but was carrying the most beautiful little baldheaded baby girl I had ever laid eyes on. She told me the baby's name was Margaret, and she let me hold you while she told me her heartbreaking situation. As a last resort, she said, she had called her mother, explained the dilemma she found herself in, and begged to return home. In between sobs, Mayme told me her mother's words, ones I will never forget. She said, 'Mayme, you and Diane are welcome to return home, but you cannot bring *that baby* with you.'" I was speechless, having trouble understanding how a mother could say those words to her own child.

"When Mayme finally composed herself, she looked directly into my eyes and asked, "Lucy, will you please take Margaret?" I don't have the courage to tell Lonnie about the ultimatum my mother gave me because there wouldn't be anything he could do about it, except grieve."

I was in total shock, but after my head stopped spinning, I asked her, "Mayme are you positive about this? Are you sure this is your only solution?" With tears in her eyes, she nodded her head yes.

"I begged her to take a little more time to rethink her decision. I even told her that Honey and I would try to find a way to supply more financial help. When none of my suggestions proved to be a satisfactory solution to her dilemma, I said, "I would love nothing more than having Margaret as my daughter, but I need to discuss this shocking request with my husband. I promise I will have an answer for you tomorrow." She nodded her head *yes*, and with tears in her eyes she walked away.

When Honey got home from work that evening, I told him about Mayme's situation and her request that we adopt you. He was ecstatic! Even though the timing was not ideal because of the war and the additional financial challenge we would be facing, we felt this was an answer to our prayers. We had always wanted a baby, but so far God had not blessed us with one.

"The next day at work, I told Mayme my husband was just as excited as I was at the prospect of adopting you and promised we would provide you with the best life we could. I asked, 'Mayme, would you allow us to adopt Diane as well?'"

"She started crying and said, "No, Lucy, I'm sorry, but I can't image the pain of losing both of my children at the same time.""

"Honey made the necessary legal arrangements with a local judge, and the next day we met in his chambers and completed the paperwork which officially made you, our daughter. It was a bittersweet moment for all of us. We were overjoyed to have you in our lives, but at the same time, we felt deep sorrow and compassion for the loss we knew Mayme was experiencing. She tearfully handed you over to me, gave me a hug, and quickly left the courtroom with Diane. I never saw nor heard from her again.

Silence hung over the room when Mama finished her story. Honey finally broke the silence by saying, "Margaret, Mama did an excellent job of telling you the heartbreaking situation your birth mother found herself in when you were born. Her sorrow, however, brought so much joy and love into our lives. Please try to understand the turmoil we have been going through all these years, struggling to tell you the truth about your birth, but not wanting to hurt you, and not wanting you to resent us for not being your biological parents."

My head was spinning from the shocking story I had just heard. I felt sorrow for my birth parents' tragic love story and for the sacrifice my birth mother faced by placing me with my adoptive family. At the same time, however, I couldn't help but feel excited about finding out I have a half-sister.

I took a deep breath and said, "Thank you both for sharing my birth story with me. I am trying my best to understand the situation my birth mother found herself in, but it's still hard for me to imagine a mother giving away her own baby. It's also quite a shock to find out I have an older sister. All I can truthfully say right now is I love you both, but I need time to sort through these new feelings, to try to shut the door on my past life as I knew it, and to somehow weave this latest information into the fabric of my present life."

Mama stood up, hugged me tightly, and said, "I understand, Baby. I'm sorry we kept this from you all these years. I think part of me was afraid if you ever looked for, and found Mayme, you might end up choosing her over me."

Honey was waiting his turn for a hug, and after I obliged, he said, "Please find it in your heart to forgive us, Margaret, and try to understand our love for you couldn't be any stronger, even if you were our birth daughter."

Retreating to my room, I lied down on the bed, stared at the ceiling, and felt totally drained of emotion. I tried to control the questions swirling around in my head. *Now that Mama and Honey had finally exposed the skeleton, why don't I feel safe and comforted? Why am I still filled with fear? What will I do with this shocking information? What exactly does the future hold in store for me now?*

CHAPTER 11

Another Storm on the Horizon

Finding myself overcome with so many conflicting emotions after Mama and Honey shared my adoption story, I was having trouble sorting them out. I decided another "Bonnye-talk" was in order. The next day at school I found her at recess and asked, "Hey, Bestie, do you have to be home at a certain time after school today? I really need to talk with you, and I thought we could stop at our special spot on the way home."

She said, "That's cool, I don't have anything else I need to do." Kay, another one of our close friends, joined us and we walked off together to our favorite spot, one of the benches under a big oak tree at the edge of the playground. Sitting down, we talked about the upcoming school dance until the bell rang to signal the end of recess.

After school, I waited for Bonnye in our usual place, by the crossing guard in front of the school, and arm-in-arm, we started walking home. She wasted no time in asking, "What happened yesterday when Honey got home? Did they tell you the details about your adoption?"

Stopping, I turned to look at her and said, "Yes, but you'll have to wait until we get to our special spot because I want to take my time telling you the whole story."

With disappointment clearly visible on her face she shrugged and said, "Okay, I guess I'll just have to wait, but my curiosity is killing me."

We walked the rest of the way to our special spot in strained silence. Finally reaching the path leading to the canal, we scooted down and sat on our self-appointed rocks. Before I even had a chance to settle down, Bonnye instantly said, "OK, I'm about to burst with curiosity, so tell me everything."

I asked, "Will you please give me a minute to catch my breath?"

Giggling, she said, "I guess I don't have a choice, do I?"

Finally feeling calm enough, I said, "Now, prepare yourself for a real shock. Before I tell you the details of my adoption, there is something even more important I want to share. I found out yesterday that I have an older half-sister, named Diane."

Bonnye sat stunned, her mouth wide open, and for once, she was speechless. I said, "Yes, that critical piece of information was a major shock to me also. Let me start at the beginning and tell you the whole story."

She finally closed her mouth, nodded her head yes, and said, "I'm dying to hear every little detail."

"Mama and Honey told me about my birth mother and father's tragic love story, set during World War II. My birth mother, Mayme, already had a daughter named Diane from her first marriage, which ended in a separation. She was not able to divorce her husband, Marty, unfortunately, because in 1940 the United States enacted the first peacetime conscription act in history. This act required all men between the ages of twenty-one and thirty-five to register with their local draft boards in case of a national emergency. Tragically in December 1941 the United States entered WII and Marty was at once shipped overseas to New Guinea before Mayme had the chance to divorce him. I just had to throw in a little history to make it more interesting."

Bonnye just rolled her eyes and looked at me.

Anyway, after Mayme and Marty's separation, she eventually met and fell in love with my birth father, Lonnie. He had also registered for the draft, and they dated until the Army called his lottery number and they assigned him to a base in Gulfport, Mississippi for basic training. Tragically, Mayme discovered she was carrying his baby just a couple of months later. She moved to Gulfport to tell him about the baby and spend time with him until the Army shipped him overseas. Job-searching, she coincidentally found a job at the same hotel where Mama worked. When finally, the Army shipped Lonnie overseas, Mayme stayed in Gulfport and tried her best to work and support both of us, but due to financial difficulties, she found it was impossible. Since Mayme and Diane had been living with her mother, brother, grandmother, and great-grandmother somewhere up north before she moved to Gulfport, she called them and asked if she could return home with her children. Being Hungarian immigrants, and extremely strict Catholics, they wouldn't allow her to return home and live under their roof with an illegitimate child. So, as a last resort, Mayme asked Mama if she and Honey would be willing to adopt me. Of course, they were ecstatic about the idea, and even tried to adopt Diane too, but Mayme refused."

Bonnye said, "Margaret, I am devastated to hear the tragic circumstances surrounding your adoption, and the fact that you have a sister you never knew about. Have you thought about what you're going to do now since you have this latest information? Do you think you are going to try to find your birth mother or Diane?"

Suddenly, I heard a loud clap of thunder! I looked up at the sky, and dark clouds signaled a storm was brewing. "Bonnye," I answered, "From the looks of this weather we better get out of here and run home as fast as we can. But, to answer your question, "No, I'm not sure what I'm going to do yet."

We made it home just before it started storming and headed straight into the kitchen to fix sandwiches. When we had our snacks and glasses of milk, Bonnye asked, "Why don't we just take our snacks to your room and finish our conversation instead of watching *American Bandstand*?"

Agreeing with her, we went to my room, sat cross-legged on my bed, and between bites of my peanut butter, banana, and mayonnaise sandwich, I said, "I've been thinking about my options since yesterday. I would love nothing more than to find Diane, but I have no idea how to begin a search. Mama doesn't even remember what state Mayme or Lonnie are from. It worries me that if I do search and find any of my birth family, the results might end up hurting Mama and Honey. I also don't think this is the best time to even think about starting a search. There is something else going on between them that I need to share with you."

Bonnye, gulping down a bite of her sandwich and almost choking, said, "I'm so sorry. I wish there were something I could do to help, but if you ever decide to start a search, you know I will do anything I can to help. Now, what is this other news about Mama and Honey?"

I said, "I think their new work routine, since they bought the car wash business, is putting too much stress on their marriage. They both seem exhausted all the time and are usually in grumpy moods. Their loud arguing awakened me at night, and I even overhead them using abusive language I've never heard them use before, talking about losing money, selling the business, and even filing for bankruptcy. So, you see why I don't feel this is a suitable time to ask them for more information about my adoption? I'm trying my best to ease the tension between them as much as possible by keeping a low profile, helping Mama more around the house, trying my best to get along better with Edith, and saying extra prayers for things to work out between them."

Bonnye, having finished her sandwich, stood up and hugged me. She said, "Margaret, I'm so sorry to hear this news about Mama and Honey. I'll say a rosary every night for them to be able to work out their business and personal problems."

I said, "Thanks, BFF. I'm sure if anything could help, it will be prayers. Why don't we play records and find a more pleasant subject to talk about?"

Bonnye headed to the record player, stacked our favorites on the spindle, and as the first one, "Rock Around the Clock" dropped on the turntable, she said, "Come on, get up off that bed, and let's dance!" By the time we had danced through "Jailhouse Rock," "Little Susie," "Yakety Yak," and Fats Domino's greatest hits, I was exhausted, but I also didn't feel as sad and stressed out as I had felt earlier.

The physical, emotional, and financial stress on their relationship, however, didn't seem to improve over the next weeks. I often overheard Mama criticizing Honey for talking her into investing their hard-earned money into a business venture. For it to now be failing and costing them even more money to keep from filing for bankruptcy, was difficult for Mama to come to terms with. After months of angry words and accusations between them, Mama and Honey finally reached a dead-end. Calling me into the living room one night for a family talk, I walked in with a sinking feeling that our prayers had not answered.

The atmosphere was stifling as we sat around with what seemed like an elephant in the middle of the room, which everyone seemed to try and ignore. Agonizing minutes later Honey finally blurted out, "Margaret, your mother and I have decided to get a divorce."

This shocking news of my parents getting a divorce shattered me and I found myself having trouble catching my breath. Honey continued, "We are losing our business, and it is my fault for making poor financial decisions. Mama and I have tried to salvage our marriage, but our efforts have failed."

Mama added, "Honey and I are both to blame for the problems we're facing. I must share the responsibility for agreeing to use our savings to start the business, and I also blame myself for not being able to put my anger and resentment aside because of it. We want you to know that our decision to end our marriage has nothing whatsoever to do with you."

Hearing her utter those ridiculous words, I jumped up and ran towards my room, yelling, "You're both wrong! Your decision has everything to do with me!" Slamming the door behind me, I flung myself on the bed and released the flood of tears I had been holding back.

Mama and Honey allowed me time alone, and a little while later I heard a soft knock on my door. I managed to find my voice and said, "Come in."

Mama walked in first and sat beside me on my bed. She said, "We're so sorry to hurt you like this, Baby. We just can't seem to find a way to work through the financial and personal problems we're facing."

I looked at her with tears running down my cheeks and the only thing I could think of to say was, "Please don't."

Honey, having followed Mama in the room, added, "Margaret, we love you so very much, but unfortunately, we just can't live with each other any longer. I promise, though, we will both be here for you whenever you need us." They each hugged me, quietly closed my door on their way out, and left me with the monumental task of picking up the pieces of my world which had just crumbled around me once again.

The next day, Honey and I tearfully said our goodbyes as he moved out of our house into his own apartment.

Struggling with this major void in our lives, Mama and I did our best to move forward without Honey. Thankfully, Mama was able to get her old job back at the same beauty shop, and instead of focusing on this major loss in my life, I tried to stay busy hanging out with my friends, playing seasonal sports, and trying to enjoy my senior year of high school.

CHAPTER 12

The 1960s

On a beautiful morning in May of 1961, I excitedly awoke, knowing today was the day I was proudly graduating from high school. I jumped out of bed, ate my favorite, French toast, Mama had made for me, bathed, and dressed. Carefully, I picked up the hanger holding my graduation gown, neatly ironed by Mama, my cap, purse, and car keys, as I was lucky enough to now own a car. Mama and Honey had given me their old 1954 Mercury Monterrey as a graduation gift. I kissed Mama on the cheek and hurried to pick up Bonnye and head to school.

As my classmates and I anxiously stood in line on the steps of St. Anthony Catholic Church, awaiting the organ cue to begin our procession, I found myself admiring a beautiful butterfly as it landed gracefully on a bluish-violet hydrangea bush on the side of the church's walkway. I remembered reading somewhere that a butterfly was a symbol of change and hope, so I said a silent prayer for this to be a good omen, one which would fulfill my wish of having both Mama and Honey here to celebrate this special day with me. Honey said he wanted to attend, but because of his new job, he wasn't sure he would be able to take the necessary time off from work. After their divorce last year, he had taken a job with the East Baton

Rouge Parish Sheriff's Department. Mama and Honey managed to maintain an unsettled relationship, as he would occasionally drop by our house for a brief visit and to have a cup of Mama's good coffee.

The organ's opening chords sounded triumphantly, abruptly returning my thoughts to the excitement surrounding me. The thirty-nine graduates of my class, clad in white caps and white gowns, slowly walked down the center aisle to the front pews of the church. As I was walking, I searched the packed church for Mama, and hopefully Honey, but had no success in finding either one of them.

The celebration of Mass was first, followed by the diploma ceremony. In the single file procession out, proudly holding our diplomas. I again anxiously searched the faces in the crowd for Mama. I finally spotted her on the righthand side of the congregation, smiling broadly and proudly wearing her new Easter hat. To my amazement, I saw Honey seated next to her, also smiling at me, and looking very handsome in his navy-blue suit and red-striped tie. The happiness at seeing them together was so overwhelming I couldn't stop the tears of joy from streaming down my cheeks and landing on the blue leather folder holding my diploma,

As our procession exited the church, family and friends rushed around, trying to find their graduate, and I spotted Mama and Honey hurrying towards me. One at a time they hugged me and said, "Congratulations, Margaret, we're so proud of you!"

After showing them my diploma, Honey said, "Mama and I want you to know we are working on our relationship and trying our best to put as much bitterness behind us as possible so we will be able to share all the other special moments in your life together as a family."

Hugging them again, I said, "Thank you both for making the effort to be here for me today and for trying to resolve your past resentments for my sake. Honey, would you like to join Mama and me in the Family Center for refreshments?" Looking at each other, they nodded their heads yes. Arms joined, the three of us walked to the reception together.

Graduation is a rite of passage into the portal of adulthood, and I had been giving serious thought during my senior year about what future path I wanted to take. During the reception, the subject of my plans came up. Honey asked, "Margaret, have you decided what you are planning to do now that you've finished high school?"

I replied, "No, not really. My close friends, like Bonnye and Kay, already have jobs, other friends are looking for jobs, and Becky is getting married. I have no interest in pursuing either of those options, so I'm thinking about going to college. The only problem is I can't make up my mind about what curriculum I want to pursue. The only career which appeals to me is that of being a physical education teacher, since I not only enjoy playing all sports, but watching them on television as well. I would love to instill that passion in young students."

Honey responded with a big smile on his face and said, "That's a marvelous idea! You have always been athletic and excelled on all the sports' teams I coached during your younger years and on your own when I gave up coaching. I certainly see you being successful if you pursued that field of study."

Mama's face, clearly not revealing a smile, tersely said, "She most certainly will not become a physical education teacher! I refuse to have a daughter of mine teaching sports. It's not a lady-like career." I understood Mama was voicing the sexist ideals of the 1960s, where a woman's place was in the home or at least working in a gender-proper job, but I was still disappointed.

Rather than continuing this discussion on my special day, I decided to appease them both by saying, "I appreciate your opinions, and I promise I will give my decision more thought. Hopefully, I can find another career to pursue that would appeal to me and meet with both of y'all's approval." My comment satisfied them, at least for the moment, and soon they were smiling again as my friends and their families surrounded us for hugs and congratulations.

CHAPTER 13

Career Decisions

Since Mama and Honey were paying for my tuition, I felt I didn't have leverage in my decision-making process. After sending for catalogues from local universities and poring over the degree programs they offered, I finally decided to enroll in the College of Business Administration at Louisiana State University in Baton Rouge. I assumed since I had taken so many clerical courses in high school, I would be well prepared for this field of study. Mama was pleased with my decision, and the next time Honey stopped by our house for a cup of coffee, I shared my news with him. I saw an expression of disappointment on his face. Off to the side, away from Mama, he told me, "Good luck, Baby. I'll support your decision, but I know your heart is in the field of physical education."

Hugging him, I said, "Thanks, Honey, but I feel this might be a good compromise."

Unfortunately, however, after struggling through one semester of tedious business administration and accounting courses, I realized the clerical courses I had taken in high school had not prepared me for this demanding and boring curriculum. Admitting to Honey he was right and explaining to Mama I had no desire to continue college, at least not in this field, and not at this time in my life, was difficult. Mama, of course, was disappointed and Honey didn't say *I told you so*, which was a blessing. Dropping out of college, however, left me feeling like a failure.

I decided to call Bonnye, who was currently working at the local newspaper office, and ask her if she knew of any job openings. She told me there was a position which had just opened in her department and said she would be happy to arrange an interview for me if I was interested. Suddenly the idea of getting a job, earning my own money, and even getting an apartment with a friend seemed appealing. I told her I was interested, so she scheduled an interview for me with her department's supervisor.

The next day, wearing my best business suit and high heels, I entered the personnel department of the *State Times-Morning Advocate Newspaper* trying to appear very self-assured, but feeling anything but confident on the inside. The interview went very well, and the supervisor offered me a job on the spot, which I happily accepted. It seemed the clerical courses I had taken in high school had finally paid off, as the skills I had learned proved to be instrumental in landing a job as an office clerk in the Classified Department. Although the starting salary was not what I had hoped for, I realized without any previous work experience, it would take time to inch my way up the pay-scale ladder.

The amazing feeling of independence, however, at earning my own money, and the freedom to make my own decisions, more than made up for the salary.

Still filled with the desire and determination to find my sister one day and discover my true ancestry, I thought maybe once I was able to move out, I might have more opportunities to conduct research on my own, without Mama and Honey finding out.

CHAPTER 14

Detours

It didn't take long for me to settle into my new work routine, and within a couple of months I had made a new friend at work named Katie. One day, while we were having lunch in the coffee shop, she asked, "Margaret, my roommate is moving out and I wonder if you would be interested in sharing my apartment with me?"

Taken by surprise, I exclaimed, "Wow, I'm not sure what to say! The idea of moving out on my own sounds exciting, but I'm not sure I can afford it. If you wouldn't mind, I would like to look at the apartment first and discuss my financial obligations before I decide."

She agreed, so we met the following weekend at her apartment. Everything about the situation was appealing. One of the things I really liked about it was the fact that it was a new apartment complex, surrounded by trees, and there was a park within walking distance. It was also just six blocks away from Mama's house, and an easy fifteen-minute drive to work. Katie and I would be able to ride together and save money on gas. The interior design of the apartment wasn't fancy, but it had all the necessary basics: two bedrooms, two baths, and a laundromat just around the corner from our apartment. Best of all, the rent was affordable.

After completing the tour, and calculating my share of the expense, I told Katie, "I love it, and I definitely want to move in, but first I have a favor to ask of you."

She said, "Name it."

I said, "Please come to my house and let me introduce you to my mother. I would love to have her blessing on my moving out, and I think she will be more agreeable if she met you first."

"Margaret, I would love to meet your mother, Katie replied. "Just let me know when it's convenient for both of you."

I thanked her, looked at my watch and said, "Mama should just now be getting home from work. If you don't have other plans, would you mind if we go now?"

Grabbing her purse, she said, "Sure, let's go! I don't have any plans this evening. I can follow you to your house, so you won't have to bring me back home."

When we arrived at my house, I unlocked the door and called out, "Mama, there is someone with me I want you to meet." As she came through the ever-squeaky swinging kitchen door, drying off her hands on her apron, I introduced Katie.

She offered a dry hand to Katie and warmly responded, "Glad to meet you, Katie. Why don't you two have a seat in the living room? I'll make us a pot of coffee, and then we can chat."

We sat down, as Mama instructed, talking about the issues at work until the aroma of the coffee preceded Mama as she came though the kitchen door. Setting the tray down on the coffee table, we fixed our cups and Mama said, "Okay, Katie, tell me about yourself."

It didn't take long for the conversation to get around to Katie's parents, and when she told us she had just recently lost her mother, Mama got teary-eyed, and insisted Katie stay for supper, so the three of us went into the kitchen to help finish the meal preparations.

During dinner, I finally brought up the subject of sharing Katie's apartment with her since her roommate had moved out.

Mama paused with her fork halfway to her mouth and slowly set it back down on her plate. Looking at me with sadness in her eyes, she said, "Margaret, I knew you would be moving out one day, but I wasn't expecting it to be so soon. If you're sure about this, however, I want you to know I support your choice of a friend to move in with. You have my blessing, and I will do whatever I can to help you both when needed."

CHAPTER 15

Disastrous Relationship

After I had moved into our apartment, Katie invited me to attend a dance with her at our local community center the next Saturday, and I accepted. While we were walking around the edges of the dance floor chatting with friends and watching the newest dance moves, I ran into Kay, one of my friends from high school. I introduced her to Katie, and my friend, Kay in turn introduced her friend, Marvin, to us.

After making small talk, Marvin asked me to dance with him, and we ended up jitterbugging the night away. Before leaving, he asked me for my phone number, and soon we began dating.

When I mentioned to Mama that I had met someone I really liked, and we had gone on a couple of dates, she said she was anxious to meet Marvin, and told me to invite him to dinner the following Friday night.

The dinner date turned out to be uncomfortable because Mama was not her usual friendly and welcoming self. We managed to get through the dinner, but on the way home, Marvin asked, "What's up with your mother, Margaret? I got the feeling she didn't like me very much."

Trying to reassure him, I said, "Mama is dealing with personal problems right now. Things have been difficult for her since she and

Honey divorced, even though they are trying to remain friends for my sake." The explanation satisfied him, but the next day I called Mama for her version.

She responded, "Margaret, all I can tell you is that I just don't have a good feeling about him. I'm sorry, but I can't seem to be able to put my finger on why I feel this way."

Following that first encounter, Mama decided to give him another chance, and she invited us for supper again. This time, however, I was the one Marvin left with an uncomfortable feeling at the end of the evening. After dinner, he and I went to my bedroom so I could take items out of my closet that I had left behind when I moved into my apartment. Marvin, looking over my shoulder, saw a box decorated with stickers on one of the shelves.

Questioning me, he asked, "What's in that box?"

I said, "Just some old mementos from middle and high school."

Despite my objection, he took the box off the shelf, opened it, and pulled out a picture of an old boyfriend, tore it up, and threw it in the trash can.

I angrily asked him, "Why in the world did you do that?"

He calmly answered, "Now that we're going steady, old boyfriend pictures are taboo."

Even though that event should have served as a warning sign, I blindly continued dating him. Then two more red flags occurred, which I again naively chose to ignore.

Honey also wanted to meet Marvin, so we met him the following weekend for dinner at the Piccadilly Cafeteria. The dinner and conversation were as equally uncomfortable as it had been at Mama's. The next day Honey called and said, "Baby, I must agree with Mama. I don't get good vibes from Marvin either."

The next red flag was that Marvin objected if I talked on the phone to Bonnye or other friends, and my phone line would be busy when he tried calling me. He also become upset if my friends asked me to go somewhere with them unless they invited him as well.

Despite the warnings, and over the objections from Mama and Honey, I stubbornly accepted his marriage proposal a year later.

Soon after, Marvin enlisted in the Navy due to the escalation of the Vietnam War, and he received orders from the Navy to report to a base in California for basic training in three weeks. He wanted us to get married before he left so I could join him there, and at other bases if he were lucky enough to remain in the United States after his training. I told him I would give it serious thought after I discussed the arrangement with Mama and Honey first, as I wanted their blessing on our marriage.

When I told Mama about our plans to get married, she said, "Margaret Ann, this is a serious matter, and I believe we need Honey present for this discussion." Because she used both my names, I knew she was anything but happy.

I nervously phoned Honey and said, "Mama thinks we need to have a family meeting to discuss the news I just shared with her. Would you be willing to meet me at Mama's tomorrow night so we can have a family talk?"

He said, "This sounds serious, Margaret, so you know very well I'll be there."

The following night, the three of us sat facing each other in the same living room where we had gathered so many other times for family talks. I began the conversation by telling Honey of Marvin's enlistment in the Navy and our plans to get married before he left for boot camp so I would be able to join him in California.

Honey's expression reflected one of the most serious looks I had ever seen on his otherwise smiling face. He said, "Margaret, please hear me out. This is a life-changing decision and I want you to try and understand my feelings about the plans you two are making. There are at least three good reasons I don't approve of your getting married so quickly. Number one, you are only nineteen, and that is still young. We want you to have every opportunity to enjoy the pleasures and freedom of your youth before you must face the responsibilities of married life. Another concern is that by moving so far away from home, you will be completely isolated, with no friends or family for support if needed. And finally, the biggest reservation I have is I don't like Marvin's jealous streak."

I felt my face turning red and responded angrily to his comment, "You don't know him like I do. He is only being protective of me."

Honey said, "Calm down, let me finish. Your mother and I have each noticed him becoming upset with you for talking to your friends or going places without him. This behavior is a warning sign that he is very controlling, and this possessiveness doesn't usually go away after marriage. Believe me, Margaret, when I was a police officer in the field, I responded to domestic-dispute calls, and the issue was usually a jealous spouse. All I'm asking is for you to give your engagement more time so you can truly get to know each other better."

Honey stopped, looked at Mama, and she nodded at him as if to say *excellent job*, and then she said, "Baby, I totally agree with everything Honey said. Please think about this very seriously before you decide."

Taking a couple of minutes to collect my thoughts, I responded, "I love you both very much and I appreciate your worrying about my welfare, but I'm a grownup now, and I can make my own decisions, with or without your blessings. Besides, neither of you know Marvin as well as I do, and I don't agree with you about the jealousy issue. I'm sure things will get better after we are married." Catching my breath, I stubbornly continued, "I don't think there is anything either of you can say to make me change my mind. So, will you please give me your blessings and agree to help me plan our wedding as quickly as possible?"

They looked at each other again and sadly shook their heads yes.

Mama, Aunt Myrtle, Uncle Neal, and Becky helped me in arranging a nice wedding very quickly. Becky offered me her beautiful wedding gown, as she had just married her high school sweetheart the previous year. Aunt Myrtle and Uncle Neal offered their home for the reception, as it was larger than ours and had a beautiful glassed-in patio in the rear of the house, and Mama took care of the cake, hors d'oeuvres and decorations.

Just a couple of weeks later, we were married in the church where I had recently graduated from high school, and we celebrated at the reception with the family members and friends who were able to attend on such short notice. We checked in to a local hotel, and two days after the wedding we boarded a plane for California.

With limited housing funds available to him to live off base, we were able to find an affordable apartment and managed to buy a very reasonable old car, which Marvin used to commute back and forth to the base. After twelve months of living in virtual solitude with no car, no friends, and no freedom, I began to think Mama and Honey might have been right about their objections. I was very lonely, with no one to talk to and nothing to do but clean our small apartment, do the laundry, cook, and watch TV.

I often thought about my sister, and my desire to search for her, but I still didn't have enough information, nor the means to conduct any research during those long, lonely days. To make matters worse, Marvin started becoming upset when I received letters from friends back home. If he found them, he would angrily tear them up and throw them away. I learned to dispose of any correspondence as soon as I read it before he returned home from the base. I thought about Honey's warning and realized I should have given serious thought to his advice. As hard as I tried, I was unable to stop Marvin's jealous rages.

Thinking things couldn't get any worse, I was sadly mistaken. I developed a medical condition and had no choice but to see one of the doctors at the infirmary on the military base. After an examination, the doctor prescribed medication, and very bluntly gave me the shocking news that he doubted I would ever be able to conceive a child. Marvin and I were both naturally shocked and disappointed, although having a baby at that point in our relationship would have been disastrous.

Our already fragile marriage deteriorated even further after this news, and a couple of months later I informed him I wanted a divorce. Although angry and resentful, he eventually agreed, and I returned home to Louisiana, hired a lawyer, and started divorce proceedings. Mama and Honey were supportive of me and my decision, and thankfully neither one ever said *I told you so.*

CHAPTER 16

Another Loss

Once again, I found myself job hunting, and I was fortunate enough to find another good clerical position at one of the local utility companies. Mama had sold the house in which I had grown up and rented a smaller house closer to her job. I moved in with her, but although I tried my best, I couldn't feel at home in her new place. I wanted to ask Mama for more details about my birth family, but I was never able to work up the courage to do so.

Experiencing so many emotional changes in my life, from finding out I was adopted, to going through Mama and Honey's divorce, to being a failure at college and then a failure in marriage, and now Mama selling the only home I had ever known, I began to wonder if I would ever feel a sense of success and security again. I also sensed Mama was feeling depressed, so I didn't want to add to her worries by asking for more information which might help me to search for my sister.

Soon after starting my new job, a couple of my co-workers invited me to join them in playing Rook in the staff lounge during lunchtime. Since we had an hour off for lunch, they used that time every day to play cards while eating their lunches. One of the members of the group, named Joy, happened to ask if anyone at the table knew of someone looking for a roommate. She explained she was presently staying with her parents since her separation from her husband but wanted to move into an apartment and needed someone to share expenses with. She said she had been looking around and found a nice two-bedroom apartment in the downtown area.

The idea of becoming independent once again piqued my interest, but I kept it to myself during the rest of the lunch hour. Later, when the opportunity presented itself, I asked my closest co-worker, Barbara, for her opinion of Joy. As it turned out, she had nothing but good things to say about her. Feeling positive about the possibility of a potential roommate, I mentioned to Joy during our game of Rook the next day that I would be interested in looking at the apartment with her. She was excited and proceeded to start telling me the positive features of the apartment complex. I loved the fact that it was in the downtown area of Baton Rouge, within walking distance of our office and the main shopping district. She asked if I would be available to look at it the next afternoon if she made an appointment with the manager and I excitedly agreed.

The next day at work I found it difficult to stay focused. My thoughts kept drifting off, thinking about the possibility of getting my own place and having the feeling of being independent once again. I was also excited because, as much as I loved Mama, I was uncomfortable living in her new house. A glimmer of hope also surfaced that somehow this move may provide an opportunity to focus on searching for my sister. I would have more freedom in conducting microfiche searches, since the library was within walking distance of the apartment complex, and I wouldn't have to report my daily whereabouts to Mama.

After looking at the apartment that afternoon, we both loved it, paid the deposit, and started making plans about moving in. Although Mama was disappointed when I told her I was moving in with a friend again, she assured me she understood and was happy that I had the opportunity to live my life freely. She also made me promise to invite Joy for dinner as soon as possible so she could meet her and "pass her blessing" on her, as she colorfully said. The next day at work I explained to Joy that Mama would like to meet her and had asked me to invite her for dinner the following weekend. Joy graciously accepted, came to Mama's house the following Saturday, and once again Mama and Joy got along beautifully. After Joy left, Mama officially gave me her blessing.

CHAPTER 17

Major Life Changes

THE 1970S

My private life underwent further major changes in 1975. A friend of mine invited me to attend a horse show with her in a nearby town. Thinking it would be fun to do something different and hoping it might take my mind off the skeleton and the frustrating search that I was still trying to conduct on my own, I accepted. While at the show, my friend introduced me to one of the competitors, named K.C. He was good-looking, polite, and talented in all the equestrian events in the show ring.

We felt an immediate attraction to each other, even though K.C.'s ancestors were all born and raised in the country, and I was a city girl. It was proof that opposites do attract. After he loaded his horses in the trailer at the end of the show, he walked over to where my friend and I were sitting and said, "It was nice meeting you, Margaret. If you wouldn't object, I would be beholden if you were to give me your phone number so I could call, and we could get to know each other better."

A new feeling of excitement flooded over me. I said, "K.C., I would like that very much. Let me write down my number, and I will be looking forward to hearing from you."

The following Thursday night K.C. called. When I answered the phone, we exchanged trivial chitchat and then he asked, "Margaret, I was wondering if you would like to go out to dinner with me Saturday night?"

I tried not to sound overly excited, so I said, "Yes, that sounds nice."

He said, "Great. I'd like to take you to a unique restaurant, named Bear Creek, which also has a Western store attached, and is in a small town close to my ranch."

I said, "That sounds intriguing, since I have never been to a Western store in my life. I'm looking forward to it."

The date was a complete hit. Not only was the food delicious, but the browsing among all the Western items I had never seen nor heard of before was interesting, and the company was perfect. Despite our different lifestyles, I discovered we had things in common, such as love of animals, similar taste in music, movies, and television shows. Most importantly, however, was the fact that I felt a peaceful and safe closeness to him that I had never experienced before.

After that amazing first date, he called to invite me to his ranch the following weekend. I accepted, of course, but I had no idea what to expect. When I arrived, I found myself feeling like I finally found a place I could happily spend the rest of my life. I loved the wide-open spaces, the ancient oak and pecan trees, acres of Bahia and Alicia grass fields dotted here and there with cows and their baby calves, and the whinnying of horses in their pens. The aroma of freshly cut grass for baling hay, hearing the hooting of owls at night, and watching the deer as they roamed in the wooded areas behind the barns, awakened my senses.

After the visit to the ranch, K.C. and I continued dating steadily for about six months before he finally popped the question one night while we were at a drive-in movie. I happily accepted his proposal, and we decided to get married as soon as we could make the necessary arrangements. When we shared the news with Mama and

Honey, they were overjoyed, as they had also taken quite a liking to K.C. Mama was a little disappointed, however, that we only wanted a small, quiet ceremony performed by a Justice of the Peace. We did agree, however, to allow our parents to give us a reception at the ranch after the ceremony.

Finally, my life was looking up, and I tried by best to convince myself I had closed the drawer on that skeleton.

CHAPTER 18

Devastating News

On a dark and dreary day in the winter of 1977, Mama called and asked if I would stop by her house after work because Honey would be there, and had news he wanted to share with us. I had been feeling that his health was failing because I noticed he had been losing weight, and his usual ruddy complexion had paled. So, with a heaviness in my heart, I went to Mama's, sensing the news would not be good. When I arrived, I gave Honey a big hug and could feel how bony his shoulders and back were. He had always been robust and solidly built, so I knew this sudden loss of weight signaled a serious condition.

Honey remained in the living room, watching television, and I followed Mama into the kitchen while she made her usual pot of coffee. She wanted to hear about my new job since I had recently started working at a large finance company, which provided me with more benefits and higher wages. When the coffee was ready, I carried the tray into Mama's tiny living room. Honey turned off the television set, and we started making small talk while we drank Mama's strong, dark roast coffee.

Finally finished with his coffee, a sudden stillness settled over the room. Honey finally said, "It breaks my heart to have to share this news with the two people I love most in the world. Since I haven't been feeling well for the last three or four months, I went to the doctor, and he ran a series of tests. I received the results a couple of days ago, and the diagnosis is late-stage esophageal cancer. My doctor sent me to an oncologist, and he told me any type of treatment would be futile."

With tears streaming down our faces, Mama and I sat in shocked silence. After regaining my composure, I said, "Honey, please get a second opinion. Have you thought about going to M.D. Anderson's Cancer Center in Houston? I hear they are innovative with their cancer research and treatments."

Choking back tears, Mama said, "Honey, there is power in prayer, and I will begin a daily Novena to St Jude, the Patron Saint of Lost Causes, and put your name on our church community prayer list as well. Please try to stay positive and keep fighting."

Honey's voice wavered as he said, "I love you both so much and I appreciate your support and prayers, but please understand I'm aware there is nothing further to be done, and I accept that."

During the next three months, I spent as much time as possible with Honey, and it was painful to see how quickly his health was deteriorating. One day I picked him up and drove him to our ranch. He had been unable to attend our reception after K.C. and I were married, so he hadn't been there before. He fell in love with the ranch and its' location at first sight, and he said, "Margaret, I'm so happy you have found someone who cherishes you as much as I do, and I love the peace and tranquility your new home provides."

I said, "Honey, I love it too, and I can't imagine ever moving back to the city."

Our visits to the ranch continued weekly until Honey became too weak to travel, and then I visited him at his apartment and later when Hospice admitted him into the hospital.

Sadly, in December of 1978, Honey passed away. As I stood under an umbrella on a very cold and rainy day, my tears mixed with raindrops, I said goodbye to the only father I had ever known and loved. Under my breath I said, "Honey, even if one day I were to find my birth father, he will never be able to replace you." Although he and Mama had been divorced for years, they had finally managed to establish a warm relationship, and she was also devastated.

Shortly after Honey's death, however, I started sensing a change in Mama's disposition. When we were together, she seemed either preoccupied or disagreeable, fussing with me over trivial issues.

After weeks of this new behavior, I decided to stop by her house after work one day and try to find the underlying cause of the problem. On seeing me, Mama hugged me and said, "Oh Baby, you must have read my mind! I have been wanting to talk to you about something that has been bothering me since Honey died."

Of course, Mama's ritual of making coffee when anyone visited had to take precedent over our conversation. When the coffee was ready, we settled down at her tiny kitchen table with our cups, and she didn't waste any time telling me what was on her mind. "Baby," she said, "Honey and I had worried about something for years, but it bothers me even more now since his death. I'm your only close family member, and since I am older than Honey was, I know I won't be around much longer. I'm aware you have K.C. in your life now, and I am incredibly grateful you found him, but nothing would bring me more comfort than to know you also had your sister in your life. So, what I am asking of you is to please search for Diane."

I sat in stunned silence as Mama asked me to do what I had been wanting to do for years but was afraid to bring up the subject. Finding my voice, I weakly asked, "Are you sure about this, Mama?"

She nodded yes, so I continued, "To be honest with you, I have been aching to find Diane ever since you told me I had a sister, but I felt by searching for her, there might be a possibility I would find one or both of my birth parents. If that happened, I didn't want you or Honey to feel threatened in any way."

Mama said, "Baby, I wouldn't feel threatened if you were to find any of your birth relatives, because I finally accepted the fact that your love for me and Honey is unconditional."

I said, "I promise I'll do my best to find her, Mama, since I am convinced, that's what you want, but it would be extremely helpful if you could give me any background information on my birth family. Do you know my birth mother's family name, what state she was born in, or where my birth father was born?"

Mama slowly shook her head no and said, "I'm sorry, but I have no idea what Mayme's family name was, and I have been wracking my brain to try and remember the state she mentioned being from. Like I said when telling you Mayme's story, I couldn't even remember the high school she told me she graduated from. I remember something about either Ohio or Illinois, but I'm not sure what, and I have no memory of Mayme ever mentioning where your birth father was from. I know this isn't help, but if you can obtain your original birth certificate, it should have the information you need to start your search for Diane. I haven't had any luck trying to find your adoption papers, but as I remember, there wasn't any other personal information about your mother."

Looking at Mama, I noticed how fragile she looked. Even though she was just seventy years old, she hadn't had an easy life. From her childhood responsibilities on the farm to standing on her feet daily as a beautician, she had endured physical challenges throughout her life. Then, by adding the weight of the traumas she had endured, from losing her life savings, her husband to divorce, and then again to death, the result was a heavy emotional burden for her to add to her already-fragile body. So, I felt determined to grant this wish before she died.

Getting up from my chair, I put my empty coffee cup in the sink and gave Mama my usual hug. As I stepped back and looked into her tired eyes, I said, "Mama, I promise I'll do my best to make this happen for you, and I will definitely keep you updated on the progress of my search."

Crying, she said, "Thank you so much for agreeing to do this, Baby. You have no idea the peace I would feel knowing you and Diane are back together again."

Driving back to the ranch, I thought about Mama's request and knew I didn't tell her there was another reason I never brought up my adoption again or the possibility of searching for Diane. Each time I thought I felt courageous enough to bring up the subject to Mama and Honey, I always found a reason why the timing wasn't right. Now that I had Mama's request and approval to search for Diane, I finally realized a couple of reasons for my procrastination all those years was the fear of what I might discover if I did find her. *Would I find more skeletons hidden away? Would I just hit dead ends and not find anything? Would she want me in her life?*

I knew any of these scenarios would have left me feeling dejected, as if I had failed again at another undertaking in my life. But finally facing reality now, I came face-to-face with the actual reason for not pursuing a search. *If I found her in my search, would my birth mother reject me again?*

CHAPTER 19

Major Decisions

After returning home to the ranch, I poured myself a cup of coffee and sat in front of the fireplace, slowly sipping the hot liquid that K.C. had brewed earlier and thought about the startling request from Mama. K.C.'s voice called out as he walked in the back door from the barn, "Sweetie, where are you?"

I answered, "Pour yourself a cup and come join me because I have some surprising news to share with you."

After he had settled down on the hearth, I began. "I stopped by Mama's after work today because, as you know, I have been worried about her since Honey died. The problem, as it unexpectedly turned out, is that she is worrying about me. She assured me that she is confident you'll take excellent care of me after she is gone but said she would be able to die more peacefully knowing I had a close blood relative in my life. So, guess what? She wants me to find Diane!"

I anxiously awaited a response from K.C. After what seemed like forever, he intently stared at me with a look of expectation on his face and said, "Well, what did you tell her?"

Letting out a loud sigh, I responded, "What else could I say, given the circumstances, except that I'll do my best to find her. On the way home, though, I finally realized the reason I have never pursued this before, although I have always wanted to find my sister. The bottom line is I am afraid of what I may find out."

Quiet settled over the room as I sipped my coffee and stared into the fireplace. K.C. finally broke the silence by saying, "I think it would be an excellent idea to search for your birth family. Regardless of what you find, you know I'll be here to help you search and will support you through the entire experience. And besides, even if you find them and they would rather not have you in their lives, you might be able to obtain valuable medical information and the names of your ancestors, which would allow you to be able to trace your genealogy like you have always wanted to do."

Thanking him, I said, "I know you're right, but somehow I feel as if that skeleton is not through tormenting me."

We continued sitting in front of the fireplace, enjoying its warmth and each other's company. K.C. finally broke the silence by asking me, "Well, did your mother give you any additional background information on your birth mother or father, such as where they were from or your birth mother's maiden name?"

Slowly shaking my head no, I said, "I'm afraid not. She doesn't have any further information. She's not even sure if the last name Mayme used at work was her birth name or the name of Diane's father. The only slight clue she gave me again was that the state of Illinois or Ohio rang a bell."

Letting out a whistle, K.C. said, "That's not very much to go on, but I guess the first step we should take is to attempt to locate your birth certificate and your adoption papers."

Agreeing that sounded like the most logical place to begin, I said, "You do remember that I don't like roller-coaster rides, don't you?

When he nodded yes, I continued, "I feel as if this search will be like that slow and terrifying approach up the first hill, and I'm scared to see what I will experience as I am plummeting down the other side. Since I do have your support though, along with Mama's request, I'm as ready as I will ever be to take the risk. So, I'll start tomorrow by checking to see how to go about getting my birth certificate and adoption papers."

CHAPTER 20

Uphill Challenges

The next day at work, during my lunchbreak, I phoned the Clerk of Court's office in Baton Rouge, inquiring how to go about obtaining my birth certificate and adoption records. I spoke with an employee who said she would be happy to provide me with the information required to obtain both records. The first question she asked me, however, was the name of the state in which I was born. When I informed her that I was born in Gulfport, Mississippi, she told me I would have to contact the Office of Vital Records office in Biloxi, Mississippi, which was the seat of Harrison County, and gave me the phone number of the agency.

Over the years I had passed through Biloxi, a neighboring city east of Gulfport, on my way to Florida for vacation getaways, so I was familiar with its' location. I called the Office of Vital Records in Biloxi, and the young lady I spoke with was very attentive when I explained my situation. I heard her take a deep breath, and with compassion in her voice, she said, "I am so sorry to have to inform you of this, ma'am but there are specific requirements which adoptees in the state of Mississippi must follow before they are able to apply for their original birth certificate. First, the adoptee must take part in a one-on-one counseling session through a social service organization, which provides post-adoption services."

Trying my best to keep disappointment and frustration out of my voice, I replied as calmly as possible, "Would you mind giving me the phone numbers of one of the agencies?"

Giving me two phone numbers, she said, "I wish you good luck in your search for your birth certificate."

Again, feeling extremely frustrated, I realized I would have to take off at least an entire day from work to travel to Biloxi, which was about a two-and-a-half-hour drive from our ranch. I decided a Friday appointment would require the least amount of time away from my job, so I asked my boss for a Friday off when I would be able to get an appointment scheduled.. With my lunch hour about over, I decided I would call one of the agencies tomorrow.

As soon as I arrived home, I took off my shoes, plopped down on the sofa in the den and tried to calm myself down. K.C. walked in from the barn minutes later and asked, "Are you okay? You sure look like you have had a rough day."

I explained the outcome of the calls I had made and asked if it would be possible for him to take a Friday off to go with me to Biloxi, and if so, did he have a preference of which Friday would work best for him? Walking over and putting his arms around me, he said, "Sweetie, I will make it a point to be available any Friday you're able to schedule an appointment."

Looking at him and seeing so much love in his eyes, I started crying and said, "I'm so lucky to have found you. I love you more than you know." We sat quietly together on the couch for a while, and then he asked if he could bring me something to drink.

I said, "Thanks, but I think I would prefer a glass of wine rather than our usual coffee." Minutes later, he returned with a glass of Chardonnay for me and a bottle of beer for himself and we toasted to success in my search.

The next day at work, again on my lunch hour, I placed a call to one of the social service agencies. Thankfully, a receptionist with a pleasant voice answered and said, "Good afternoon, please let me know how we can be of assistance to you." Feeling an immediate sense of relief, I explained my situation and she replied, "Ma'am, we do happen to have an opening on Friday afternoon of next week with Dorothy, one of our social workers."

I said, "That sounds perfect. I would appreciate your scheduling me for that day and time."

Thanking her, I hung up the phone and instantly called K.C. to share the good news and confirm the date with him. He said he would check the schedule at the barn and call me back as soon as possible. Within fifteen minutes he called to assure me he would have no problem arranging that day off.

The following Friday, we left early for our three-hour trip to Biloxi and arrived a couple of hours before my scheduled appointment. We decided to go to a cafe, which was located next door to the social worker's office and offered a stunning view of the Gulf of Mexico. We sat at an outside table, silently sipping our iced tea, with my thoughts focused on the upcoming appointment. K.C., sensing my apprehension, tried to reassure me. "You'll do fine, Sweetie, just try to relax and be yourself."

The waiter interrupted us by serving a side salad to go with the bowls of crawfish etouffee we had ordered. After finishing our delicious meal, we ordered one piece of pecan pie to share, along with a cup of coffee each.

We resumed our conversation, brainstorming about what other options might be available for us to pursue if this appointment didn't supply positive results. Looking at my watch, I told K.C. it was time for my appointment, so we paid the bill, moved the car next door, and walked in together.

A pleasant middle-aged receptionist graciously greeted us. She handed me a pen, a clipboard with a two-page questionnaire form attached and escorted us to an adjoining room with a table, two chairs, and a couch. K.C. took a seat on the couch as I sat at the table, picked up the pen and started completing the forms. Aware of my palms sweating. I discreetly wiped the perspiration on my polyester bell-bottom pants and continued. When I had completed the forms, I returned them to the receptionist and sat down on the couch next to K.C. Sitting quietly, I found myself silently saying the rosary. I had almost completed it when the receptionist walked in and asked me to please follow her.

"Wish me luck!" I said to K.C.

He squeezed my hand, winked at me, and said, "You got it!"

The receptionist escorted me into the social worker's office and gave me a seat on the opposite side of her desk. At once I caught the scent of my favorite perfume, Charlie, wafting from the attractive young lady as she stood up, shook my hand, and introduced herself as Dorothy Thomas. As we both sat down, I caught myself admiring her appearance as she was looking over the papers I had filled out. She was dressed in a baby blue cowl-neck sweater, accenting the blue in her grayish-blue eyes, a tan colored slim skirt, and wore her hair in the newest wedge cut.

After skimming through the papers, she started the conversation by saying, "Margaret, as I take notes, I want you to tell me any background information about yourself that you would like to share, and what brought you in today."

I started with the discovery of a skeleton in the drawer and ended by explaining my hope that she would be able to help me find my sister.

When I finished telling my lengthy story, Dorothy said, "Margaret, I know you must be exhausted after having to relate the emotional experiences you have gone through, so I suggest we take a little break, have a cup of tea, coffee, or soda, and let you relax a bit."

Getting up from her desk, she walked over to a credenza where she had two large urns on display, one contained coffee, and the other one held hot water for the vast variety of teas she had displayed in a pewter bowl. Next to the table was a small refrigerator stocked with bottles of chilled water. Asking me for my preference, I said, "I think I'll just have a bottle of water, thanks."

She returned to her desk with a cup of coffee and started a conversation about Hurricane Camille, the devastating hurricane in 1969 that caused over five billion dollars in damage along the Mississippi Gulf Coast, particularly in Gulfport and Biloxi. She said, "Margaret, the courthouse was heavily damaged, along with the destruction of too many vital records to count, which has caused countless problems for those searching for legal documents. It's only fair that I warn you of this possibility if I search for your birth certificate. I also need to explain the Mississippi state process that adoptees must follow when attempting to obtain their original birth certificate. First, the state seals the birth certificates of all adoptees. This means that if your birth parents did not attach a release form to your original birth certificate, the state would not allow us to release it to you, nor any of the information recorded on it,

"Taken aback by the news Dorothy just shared with me, I interrupted, "So, let me get this straight. You are saying that the state will not allow me to have access to my own birth certificate? If my mother did not attach a release form, what would happen next?"

Sipping her coffee, Dorothy continued. "Yes, Margaret, I'm afraid that is the law. I have the authority to obtain your original birth certificate, and when I receive it, I will inform you as to whether your birth mother attached an authorized release. If she didn't, all I can do is confirm the information you have in your possession is the same as the information recorded on your birth certificate.

If you wish to pursue this further, the first step is for me to prove you are emotionally stable enough to accept any outcome that may occur because of my search. If I can obtain your birth certificate, and there is a release form attached there may be negative outcomes if you were able to contact one or both of you birth parents. It's always possible that one or more of your immediate family may not want you back in their lives, one or both of your parents may be deceased, and, on occasion, the search may be unproductive. To enable me to arrive at an assessment of your emotional stability to manage any of these possibilities I would ask you a series of questions and I would require you to analyze and interpret various pictures. The test results would provide me with the information needed to access your emotional stability. Now that I have explained the entire procedure, Margaret, do you still want to move forward with the search?"

A wave of disappointment, frustration, and confusion rushed over me, and I found myself on the verge of tears. Taking time to compose myself, I answered, "Go ahead with your analysis, Dorothy, and if the test results indicate I am emotionally able to manage what is discovered, I would like for you to order my birth certificate."

Dorothy acknowledged with a nod of her head and said, "Okay, then let's get started!"

An exhausting hour later, after answering situational and multiple-choice questions and looking at pictures and slides to assess my reactions, Dorothy responded, "Well, Margaret, we have concluded the test. Try to relax while I tally the results."

After what seemed like hours, she said, "Margaret, looking at your test results, I have absolute confidence in your emotional stability. The tests overwhelmingly reveal you have the inner strength to manage any information I might share with you. So, I will order your birth certificate tomorrow and call you as soon as I have it in my possession. Do you have any further questions?"

Feeling physically and emotionally drained, I slowly lifted myself out of the chair, and on shaky knees, I stood up and said, "None, that I can think of at the moment."

I followed her to the door, where we shook hands and she said, "It was very nice meeting you, Margaret, and I wish you the best of luck in your search."

Thanking her, I responded, "It was nice meeting you as well, Dorothy, and I will anxiously await your phone call."

Returning to the lobby, K.C. was still sitting on the sofa, working on his crossword puzzle in the book he always carried around with him. He got up, looked at me, and said, "From your expression, it doesn't look as if you received good news."

I said, "Let's drive around a little, maybe take a walk on the beach to clear my head, find a place where we can get a bite to eat, and then I'll give you the details."

He nodded his head in agreement and we drove in silence down the beach highway until we found a public parking area, got out of the car, and walked together on the beach. Taking my shoes off, I walked in the refreshing surf, breathed in the smell of the salty air, and found the sounds of the waves washing on the shore very soothing. Finally, I stopped, faced K.C. and said, "I'm feeling better and I'm getting hungry. Are you ready to go?"

He said, "That sounds good to me. I'm in the mood for oysters. Let's rinse the sand off our feet at the public faucet, and we'll drive around until we spot a place that serves them. We drove about a mile and spotted a cute little seafood restaurant advertising "Fresh Gulf Oysters" and decided to try it.

After K.C. and I sat down in a booth and one of the wait staff took our order, I started telling him the details of the meeting with Dorothy. He was as shocked as I had been, and he said, "Well, all we can do is hope and pray she thought about doing that. We know Larry didn't because he wasn't even in the picture when she allowed your parents to adopt you. If she didn't attach a release, we'll just have to find other ways of searching for your sister."

Nodding my head in agreement, we turned our attention to the luscious oyster trays that the waiter had just placed in front of us.

CHAPTER 21

Ups and Downs on the Roller Coaster

After returning home from Biloxi, I visited Mama, as promised, to share the information I had obtained. Obviously disappointed, she said, "Baby, please don't let this failure get you discouraged. I've been saying novenas that you will find Diane, and I have faith that God will answer my prayer."

Thanking her for the prayers I asked, "Mama, is there a chance you've remembered anything else Mayme might have told you which could give us a hint of where to search for her?"

Shrugging her shoulders, she said, "I have been trying my best to remember, but nothing else has come to mind."

I said, "Please don't stress yourself out trying to remember. Maybe if you just let it go, something may trigger your memory when you least expect it. In the meantime, though, while waiting to hear back from Dorothy about my birth certificate, I'm going to start my own search. Who knows what I might find? All I want you to do is just keep saying your novenas."

Hugging each other goodbye, I promised to keep her posted on anything I discovered.

Since affordable home computers were not available until the early 1980s, and search engines were not in existence until 1990, the only means available for me to conduct family research in 1979 was by using census records on microfiche. Mama had introduced me to this tool years ago when she helped me construct the ancestry tree for my social studies project. Microfiche is a transparent 35mm film which reproduces printed pictures such as census records, burial sites, and newspaper clippings in miniature form. The Family History Library in Baton Rouge had the largest collection of census records in our area, as it is a branch of the Mormon Library in Salt Lake City, Utah, the largest genealogical library in the world.

Armed with what little information we had, K.C. and I began frequent trips to search through old census records. We began by approximating the year my birth grandparents might have been born and started searching for the last names of my birth mother and father in the states of Illinois and Ohio since those were the two states Mama seemed to remember. Each time we finished with one census year, we returned them to the clerk and asked for another year. Handing us each a sheet of microfiche, which the library protected in a plastic sleeve, the clerk good-naturedly said, "Good luck, maybe this one will give you the information you're searching for."

Thanking her, K.C. and I moved to a viewer, removed the film from the sleeve, and carefully slid it through the microfiche reader and began reading each name on the film. Since the process was obviously tedious, we took frequent breaks, walking upstairs to the coffee shop to have a drink or a bite to eat. After we felt mentally alert again, we walked back downstairs and continued our search. After weeks of this frustrating routine, we finally decided to give up. Besides being time-consuming, it had also proven to be unproductive. The only remaining thread of hope I still clung to was there would be a letter of release from my birth mother attached to my birth certificate.

A week later, as I walked in the front door from work, I heard the telephone ringing. Throwing down my purse on the couch, I ran as fast as I could to the kitchen to answer it. Breathlessly, I said, "Hello."

Dorothy jokingly said, "Hello, Margaret. It sounds like you just finished running a marathon. Why don't you take a little time to catch your breath?"

After I had composed myself and was breathing as normally as possible under the circumstances, I said, "Hi, Dorothy. Thank you. I'm okay now, given the fact that I have been waiting for this call for what seems like forever."

"Margaret," she said, "I'm holding your original birth certificate in my hand, but I'm so sorry to tell you there is no release from your birth mother attached to it."

With an immediate sinking in my stomach, like the feeling you get when topping the highest incline on a roller-coaster just before the fear of catapulting down, I struggled to regain my composure. The disappointment and feeling of unfairness that Dorothy was able to look at something so vitally personal and important to me filled me with anger and envy. Trying my best to settle down from the virtual stomach-turning roller-coaster ride, I asked Dorothy, as calmly as possible, "So, is there anything else we can do except your verifying the information I already have?"

Dorothy compassionately responded, "I'm afraid not, Margaret. If you tell me each piece of information you have, I can only respond yes or no if it's a match to the data on your birth certificate."

Taking a deep breath, I began, "My mother's name is Mary Woodard."

Dorothy replied, "Yes, that's correct."

Continuing, I said, "My father's name is Lonnie Belluga."

Again, she replied, "Yes, that's correct."

We continued like this with each piece of information I had obtained from my baptismal certificate, with Dorothy replying "yes" to each one.

Finally, just going by Mama's faint memory of where Mayme may have been born, I said, "I think Mary was born in Illinois."

For the first time, there was hesitation, and Dorothy replied, "No, that's not correct."

With a sinking in my stomach, I struggled to catch my breath and continued. "My adoptive mother thought she remembered her being from either Illinois or Ohio."

Once again Dorothy sadly replied, "No, Ohio is not correct either." She paused, and said, "Margaret, please try to understand that I'm not allowed to let you go through each state one by one."

Trying my best to prove to her I was indeed emotionally capable of managing the information she provided, I replied as calmly as possible, "Thank you for your efforts, Dorothy, and I do understand that the state has your hands tied. Would you by chance have any other suggestions as to how I might be able to continue searching for my sister with such limited information?"

She said, "Margaret, I regret that I'm not aware of any other resources available to you at this time, but I'll check around, and if I discover anything which may be of help, I will certainly let you know. I have heard that there may be changes in the future as to the laws governing adoptee's searches for their birth parents. I know other states are already loosening the criteria. I wish you the best of luck, and if you receive any other information, please call me and I will be happy to compare it to your birth certificate."

Thanking her again, we hung up.

Devastated by the news I had just received from Dorothy, I considered giving up. As much as I wanted to find my sister, discover my true ancestry, and grant Mama's wishes, I was not sure I was as emotionally capable of pursing the search as Dorothy had assessed me to be.

K.C. was already in the kitchen, just coming in from the barn, so I ran into his arms and burst into tears, sharing with him the gist of the conversation with Dorothy.

Consoling me, he said, "Let's go sit down. I want to hear all the details."

Sitting together in the sunroom, I managed to gather my thoughts and tell him everything that had happened. I knew I also had to share this upsetting news with Mama, but I didn't want to tell her on the telephone. I asked K.C. if he would mind picking her up if she was able to come for dinner, and spend the night. Of course, he agreed.

Calling her, I asked, "Mama, have you eaten yet?

She said, "No, I haven't. Why?

I replied, "I have gumbo and K.C. offered to pick you up to come have supper with us and spend the night."

"Margaret, she said, I know you have news you don't want to tell me on the phone, but I would enjoy seeing y'all and gumbo sounds delicious."

I quickly thawed out a container of andouille and chicken gumbo I had in the freezer, put garlic bread in the oven, tossed a salad, and set the table. By the time K.C. and Mama arrived, I was ready to serve supper.

I said, "Why don't we sit down and eat while the food is hot, and I'll fill you in on the details of the searches K.C. and I have been conducting, and about the telephone call I received today, after we've finished supper?" Mama reluctantly agreed, which made K.C. happy since he had been too busy to eat lunch today.

After we were through, I stacked the dishes in the sink, and I made another pot of coffee. We made our way to the den, engaging in small talk, and settled down, enjoying the pungent aroma of the coffee.

Calming down enough to update Mama, I began with the search of census records K.C. and I had unsuccessfully conducted. Then I continued by explaining the appointment with the social worker, the Mississippi law that requires consent from the birth mother to release information on the birth certificate to an adoptee, the tests

Dorothy had conducted to determine my emotional stability, and concluded by informing Mama that since Mayme had not left a consent form on my birth certificate I was unable to obtain any new information other than to confirm she was not from Ohio or Illinois.

Mama was understandably upset, and she said, "Baby, I'm so sorry you are reaching one dead end after another. I blame myself for not having asked Mayme for more information about her and Lonnie's family backgrounds. You need to give yourself a break and put the search on hold for a while. Try to focus on something else, and in the meantime, I will continue my novenas for answers."

Getting up to refill Mama's coffee cup, I said, "I love you for saying I should take a break right now, because I know how much this means to you, but I think you're right."

Trying to take my mind off the skeleton, which was obviously still haunting me, I tried my best to get involved in other projects, without success. I realized I was unable to stop obsessing over finding my sister. If I were not constantly brainstorming innovative searching ideas, I found myself fixated on how it would play out if I did find Diane one day. My mind reeled with questions: *What does Diane look like? Does she like to do the same things I do? Is she married? Do I have nieces and nephews? Does she work? If so, what does she do? Do we have any other sisters or brothers about which I don't know? Does she know about me? If so, why hasn't she searched for me? If I find her, will she tell me she doesn't want me in her life?* Realizing I was unable to get off this roller coaster, I wasn't sure where to go from here.

CHAPTER 22

Temporary Side-Track

After K.C.'s father retired, he and K.C.'s mother decided to invest in a business venture which required a great deal of bookkeeping and were looking for someone to manage the financial records. Since they were aware that my occupation as a customer service representative was stressful and had been affecting my physical and emotional health, as well as my personal relations with others, they offered me the position. In addition to flexible work hours and the ability to work from home, they also offered me a generous salary. After giving their offer thoughtful consideration, and with K.C.'s and Mama's blessings, I decided to accept their offer. Still having a desire to obtain a college degree, I realized that by working part-time, I would also have the opportunity to enroll as a part-time student. Still filled with doubts and anxiety, however, I resigned from my job and sadly said goodbye to the co-workers who had also become close friends.

After speaking with a career counselor at Louisiana State University, I decided, with her aid, to enroll in an undergraduate curriculum in elementary education, followed by a master's degree program in school counseling. Although this was not my original goal of being a physical education teacher, I had aged quite a bit since high school so I didn't think a physical education career would be the most practical pursuit at this time in my life. I was interested in the counseling program, as I felt it would still allow me to affect children in a positive way, only I would be teaching them life and coping skills, rather than physical education skills.

Besides keeping myself busy with my studies and my part-time bookkeeping job, I also travelled with K.C., as often as possible, when he competed in local or out-of-state horse shows. Over the years, we had formed close relationships while travelling on the horse show circuit and we always looked forward to visiting with our friends when there was a show in their area. While travelling, I discovered I had picked up a habit of checking the phone book in each hotel room and searching through it for the last name of each of my birth parents recorded on my baptismal certificate, but unfortunately never had any luck in finding either last name

The longing to know my true genetic identity was still preoccupying my thoughts even though I hadn't discovered any other official way to search for my birth family. Trying my best to control this impulse, I found I would succeed for a while, and then the obsession would take over again. The skeleton would stick an arm or leg out of that drawer and remind me of my traumatic discovery so many years ago.

CHAPTER 23

Boarding the Roller Coaster Again

K.C. and I were watching a crime drama on television the next week and one of the characters hired a private investigator to locate someone in their family who had been missing. Suddenly, a light bulb came on in my head, and I blurted out, "K.C., That's it! Why haven't we thought about hiring a private investigator? Honey, working in the police department, often talked about cases involving missing persons."

K.C. turned off the television set and we discussed the pros and cons of pursing this possibility. Other than the expense which would be involved, the probability of another dead end, and the fact that neither of us knew any private investigators, we agreed we should at least try it.

The next day I called Mama, explained what we were considering, and asked her opinion.

"That's a great idea, Baby. I can't imagine why neither one of us thought about it before."

With excitement building, I asked her, "Do you happen to know of a detective or a former officer on the police force with Honey who does private investigative work, or maybe remember Honey mentioning someone?"

She paused. "I'm having trouble remembering any names right now, but let me think about it, and if I can't remember anyone, I'll call some old friends, whose husbands was on the police force with him, and see if they know of someone who is doing private investigative work. I'll let you know as soon as possible."

Thanking her, we said goodnight. I suddenly found myself feeling apprehensive as I imagined myself once again creeping higher up on the steep incline of a roller coaster.

A couple of days later, Mama called and said, "I have good news, Margaret. One of my old friends happened to remember the name of a retired police officer who is now a private investigator."

Jotting down the name on a notepad I kept by the phone, I said, "Thanks so much, Mama. Now, keep your fingers crossed and keep saying your novenas that this will provide the answer we've been looking for. I promise to keep you updated."

Hanging up the telephone, I reached for the phone book in the slot under our telephone desk at home and searched the Yellow Pages under the heading of Private Investigators. At the bottom of the second page, an advertisement's slogan read, "Need help? Let Duke fight for you!" The remaining information included the name of the investigator Mama had given me, Roddy Duke, his address, phone number, and positive reviews of his service from former clients.

With trembling fingers, I dialed the listed number. A very efficient female voice answered, "Duke's Private Investigators, how may we help you?"

My stomach was doing flips, but I managed to keep a steady, businesslike voice and asked, "May I please speak to Mr. Duke?

The receptionist said, "I'm sorry, ma'am, he is out of the office at the moment, but I will be happy to give him your name and phone number and have him return your call as soon as possible." I gave her the requested information, thanked her, and hung up, hurrying to school for my afternoon class.

As I returned home that afternoon, thinking about the upcoming venture, the anxiety of boarding another emotional roller coaster terrified me, and I wasn't sure I was brave enough to board one again. Arriving home, I looked at the answering machine as I walked through the kitchen, but the red light, indicating a new voice message was not blinking. I walked out to the barn to look for K.C. and found him in the feed room.

When he saw me, he stopped what he was doing and asked, "Is something wrong, Sweetie?"

I asked, "I'm just curious if maybe you had answered the phone and taken a message for me?"

He answered, "No, why?"

I said, "Go ahead and finish feeding the horses. It's not critical, so I'll explain when you come in. I'm going to make a pot a coffee and meet you in the kitchen in a little while."

After I got the coffee pot started and changed my clothes, I returned to the kitchen, poured our coffee, and had just sat down at the table when K.C. walked through the back door. He took off his boots, put on his house shoes, washed his hands, gave me a kiss, and sat down next to me.

"Okay, now tell me what's going on. Something has your face filled with anxiety."

I said, "Mama called me this afternoon and gave me the name of a reputable private investigator that used to work with Honey at the police department before he retired. I called his office, but he was out, and I'm waiting for him to call me back."

After engaging in more casual conversation about his day, I got up from the table and busied myself cooking supper.

Later, as I was working on a school assignment, the telephone rang, and I quickly ran to answer it.

A man's booming voice startled me as he said, "Hello, Ms. Altazin, this is Roddy Duke. I'm sorry to call so late, but I've had a busy day. I hope you don't mind." Assuring him it was perfectly fine, he continued,

"When my receptionist gave me your message, I wondered if you just might happen to be related to Arthur Altazin?" I told him I was his daughter and related the story of his retirement and his death.

He said, "I'm so sorry to hear that. I had profound respect for him. So, please tell me how I may be of service to you, Ms. Altazin."

I said, "Please call me Margaret. Well, it's a long story, but I will do my best to just give you an abbreviated version right now. When I was ten years old, I accidentally discovered that Mama and Honey, the name I called my father, had adopted me when I was three months old. It wasn't until years later that I confronted them with my shocking discovery, and they informed me I have a maternal half-sister. My adoptive mother, Lucy, and I, would like to locate her, but I haven't had any luck searching on my own.

He responded, "Margaret, I would be happy to take your case, but before you decide if you want me to proceed, I need to explain the process that would be involved. First, you would have to come to my office and complete the necessary legal documents, sign a contract, and pay my retainer fee. Once you complete the requirements, I would conduct an interview with you to obtain the information about your adoption and the research you have attempted. Do you want more time to think about it, or would you like for me to make an appointment now?"

Only briefly hesitating, I said, "I am in agreement with your terms, so please go ahead and schedule an appointment for me."

"Okay then, let me check my calendar," he said. I heard him flipping pages, and he finally responded, "Margaret, I happen to have a late afternoon appointment Tuesday of next week at 4:00."

I said, "That's perfect. I'm going to LSU now and I don't have classes on Tuesday afternoons."

He responded, "Great! Let me give you directions to my office and I'll see you next week."

Jotting down the directions, I said, "Thank you so much for considering my case, Mr. Duke."

He responded, "My pleasure, Margaret. I'm looking forward to meeting you, and I hope I can bring closure to your search."

The following Tuesday, I left home a little earlier than necessary just in case I had a problem finding Roddy Duke's office. Following his directions, I was pleasantly surprised to find his office in an old Victorian home, which the owner had renovated into a duplex, housing a law firm on one side and Mr. Duke's Detective Agency on the other. The house, perched atop a small hill, was in the historic downtown district of Baton Rouge, surrounded by ancient moss-strewn oak trees, and overlooked the Mississippi River.

As I entered his charming office, I heard the old hardwood floorboards creaking under my feet as I walked up to the receptionist's desk. A young, college-aged girl was sitting behind an antique rolltop desk. She looked up at me through her round, tortoiseshell glasses and said, "Good afternoon. How may I help you?"

I said, "I have an appointment with Mr. Duke at 4:00, but I'm a little early."

She responded, "Of course, you must be Ms. Altazin. Please have a seat in the foyer. He will be with you shortly."

I chose to sit on an antique love seat, took a magazine from the round, oak coffee table and was leafing through the pages when a rotund, bald man approached me, appearing to be in his sixties. He extended his hand, and with a powerful grip he shook mine and introduced himself as Roddy Duke.

I said, "Pleased to meet you, Mr. Duke."

He said, "I remember you, Margaret, but as a tiny little cotton-topped girl, playing with your toys on the floor in your daddy's office at the police station. I must say you have certainly grown into a beautiful young woman, and I want to extend my condolences once again on the death of your father. He was a fine man and an outstanding Assistant Chief of Police. Now, shall we go into my office?"

Nodding yes, I followed him, and passing by the receptionist, who stood facing us at a coffee nook on one side of her desk, she asked me, "Would you care for a cup, Ms. Altazin? If so, how do you like yours?"

I said, Thanks, I would. I take mine black, with two sugars, please."

After pouring the coffee, she handed us each a cup, and we made our way into the detective's office. He shut the door behind us as we walked in and showed me to a chair opposite his desk. We started with small talk about the weather and our common interest in LSU sports until we had finished our coffee. Then he asked, "Okay, Margaret, are you ready to get down to business?"

With butterflies in my stomach, I answered, "I guess I'm as ready as I'll ever be."

He said, "First let me explain my fees. You will have to pay my retainer fee, which is five hundred dollars today, and my hourly fee is forty dollars, plus any travel expenses, such as gas or hotels if I must travel out of town."

I said, "I understand, and I'm prepared to pay your retainer fee today."

He reached into his middle desk drawer and pulled out a couple of long, legal papers. Turning them around to face me, he handed me a pen and said, "The first step is for you to complete this questionnaire."

"Certainly" I said. I proceeded to answer the questions on the forms and gave them back to him.

After looking them over, he handed me a contract. Reading it with me, he said, "Now, I need your signature on the bottom line if you are in agreement with the terms."

Responding, "I agree, Mr. Duke," I signed the document and handed it back to him. Calling his receptionist from an intercom on his desk, she walked in, took the documents, made Xerox copies, returned to his office, and handed me a copy of the paperwork.

"Now, Margaret," he said, "I'd like for you to fill me in on everything you know about your adoption and explain the searches you have tried."

I started with that fateful day I found the skeleton in the drawer, described my confrontation with Mama and Honey, and concluded with the all the failed efforts from my searches. After I finished my story, I waited for a reaction from him.

He was sitting back in his chair, twiddling his thumbs on his belly, and he appeared to be miles away. His booming voice startled me when he finally said, "I have had my tape recorder on while you were talking, Margaret, so I am able to remember all the details you shared with me. Honestly, I'm afraid this is not very much information to begin a search with, but I do have resources which may prove to be helpful. I promise I'll try my best to find your sister and I will keep you informed of my progress by telephone. Please understand, however, I cannot guarantee you anything."

Feeling downcast, I was aware it was impossible for him to promise me he would find Diane, but I replied, "I understand this is a next-to-impossible task, Mr. Duke, but I appreciate your taking my case in spite of that."

Standing, he walked around his desk, we shook hands, and he showed me to the door.

The following Monday, after returning home from school, I saw the red light blinking on our answering machine. I pressed the "play" button and at once recognized the familiar voice.

"Margaret," he said, "this is Roddy Duke, I think I have uncovered information relevant to your case, but I would prefer it if you were to come to my office so I can share it with you in person. Please call my office tomorrow morning and let me know what day would be convenient for you to come by."

Not sure if I was feeling more excited or scared, I had the same "heart in my throat" feeling as when I neared the top of another notorious roller coaster. I couldn't help wondering if this "ride" might finally provide the answers I had been searching for.

Sleep didn't come easy that night, and the first thing I did the next morning, even before making coffee, was call the detective saying "Good morning, Mr. Duke, this is Margaret Altazin, and

I received your message. I can come by your office after class this afternoon, if that will be convenient for you."

Answering, "Good morning to you also, Margaret. Let me check my calendar. A minute later he said, "I just happen to have a cancellation this afternoon, so I'll look forward to seeing you about four o'clock."

After an apprehensive day at school, I arrived at his office early. The receptionist informed me that Mr. Duke was still in a conference with his earlier client and would be with me as soon as possible. Trying my best to relax, my mind drifted off to where this information might take me on the long and tedious journey I had been travelling on.

Lost in my thoughts, his booming voice startled me when he said, "Sorry to keep you waiting, Margaret. Please let's go into my office."

Again, he started with casual conversation, obviously trying to put me at ease. Then he opened the file on his desk, and said, "Margaret, I'm afraid I have discovered discouraging news on both sides of your biological family. The first thing I discovered is the death of a man years ago, whom I believe to have been your birth father. I would need to conduct further research, however, and travel to Michigan to confirm this. Also, records of a fatal private plane crash years ago, also in Michigan, reported that the pilot, with the same last name as your birth mother's, was flying the plane. The only passenger was a young woman named Diane, with no last name given, who would have been about the same age as your sister. I'm so sorry to report this tragic news, but as I said, there is no way for me to be certain this was your sister unless I travel to Michigan, conduct more research and interviews with local officials in the area. I'll be happy to continue searching, but I must inform you it would require quite a bit of additional expense to cover my travels."

Feeling as if Mr. Duke's news had been a kick to the stomach, I did my best to compose myself. "Mr. Duke, I can't thank you enough for your empathy and challenging work. For the time being, however,

I think I'll decline further research. I need time to consider all the possibilities, including the most logical one of calling off my search completely. And right at this moment, I don't feel as if I am able to arrive at any rational decisions."

He stood up and said, "I totally understand, Margaret, but if you ever decide to pursue it again, please let me know. I wish you all the luck in the world in locating news about your sister, and I hope you will be able to come to terms with the disappointing news I just shared."

After leaving his office and arriving home, I was relieved to see K.C. at the barn with a client. At that moment, I wasn't in the mood to discuss the meeting with anyone. I went straight to our room, put my things down on the bed, and decided to take a hot shower. The pulsating water loosened the tight muscles in my body, and when I stepped out, I felt a little more relaxed.

Walking into the kitchen, K.C. was just coming in the back door. He looked at me and said, "I don't like the expression on your face. Go sit down and relax in the recliner in the den. You look as if a glass of wine would be in order this evening."

I was sitting down in the recliner, petting Liza, one of our cats who jumped up on my lap, lost in thought about the disappointing outcome of my meeting when K.C. returned with my glass of wine.

He said, "Anytime you're ready to talk is fine. No rush!" After sipping my Chardonnay, I said, "Well, it seems Mr. Duke did discover some critical information on individuals who could possibly be my birth relatives; however, none of it was good."

I shared all the details of his search, and when I finished, K.C. said, "I know I'm still being optimistic, but he did admit he can't confirm those people were your birth family members unless he digs deeper into the facts. You need to step back from this whole search for a while and see how you feel. You don't need to decide anything today.

Nodding my head in agreement, I thanked him for his practical input, and then I started thinking about having to share this news with Mama. I knew I didn't want to tell her over the phone, so I decided I would stop by her house the next day on my way to school and share the upsetting news with her in person.

I left earlier than usual for class the next morning, and mustering all my courage, I stopped at her house. As soon as she opened the door, I could tell she already had a premonition of why I was there. Hugging me, she said, "Baby, I can see in your eyes that something is wrong. I'm guessing you didn't get good news from Roddy Duke's investigation. Sit down and tell me about it."

I sank down on her couch and as difficult as it was, I managed to share the details of the traumatic discoveries Mr. Duke had found.

When I finished, I could see she was disappointed, but she surprised me when she said, "Please, don't give up, Margaret. I keep telling you I have a strong feeling you will find Diane one day, and I can't bring myself to believe she was the one who died in that plane crash. I'm not sure how I feel about the man Roddy Duke thinks may have been your deceased birth father, but even if that information were to be true, I don't think he would have been any help in finding your sister."

Mama's compassionate and optimistic reaction moved me to tears. We hugged each other, and I said, "Mama, I can't make you any promises, other than to say I will consider your suggestion."

CHAPTER 24

Happenstance

I continued trying to come to terms with the fact that Diane was dead, but my conversation with Mama left me with nagging doubts. An opportunity to address those doubts presented itself in 1995. K.C. had to travel to Texas to deliver a horse to a friend's ranch, and since I happened to be off from school due to it being a local holiday, I was able to go along with him. After arriving at their ranch, Chuck, Sandy, and K.C. completed the business part of our trip, and we decided to go to a cafe for dinner. Upon arrival of out drinks, Chuck announced that he would like to make a toast. Raising our glasses, he said, "To my wife, Sandy, for finally locating her birth mother, as well as three sisters!"

We clinked glasses, and almost dropping mine, I managed to say "Cheers!" with the rest of them. Struggling to regain my composure, I finally took a sip.

I said, "Sandy, I had no idea your birth parents had placed you for adoption. I 'm particularly interested in hearing the details of how you were able to locate your birth mother, since the opportunity has never presented itself for me to tell you that I am also an adoptee."

Sitting back in her chair, Sandy said, "Wow, what a coincidence! I'll be more than happy to tell you my story while we are enjoying our drinks and appetizers.

As the server placed two baskets of nachos and bowls of various dips on the table, she began. "When I was four years old my parents told me they had adopted me from an orphanage in Arkansas. My being adopted didn't really bother me, and I wasn't curious about finding my birth mother, and there was no record of my birth father's name. However, a couple of months ago my family doctor diagnosed me with breast cancer, and the oncologist informed me that my medical history would be extremely helpful in deciding my best treatment options, and I told him I would do my best to search for my birth mother. The first step I took was to apply for my original birth certificate. The County Clerk's office in Arkansas informed me that the state seals all adoptees' birth certificates and access to them is not possible unless the parents had attached a written release form. Of course, I was disappointed to learn that my mother had not attached a release form to mine."

Empathizing with her, I said, "I totally understand how you felt, Sandy, since I had the same experience. I'm sorry to interrupt. Please go on."

She continued, "That's okay, Margaret. Well, since my adoptive mother had given me the name of my birth mother before she died, in case I ever wanted to find her, I started searching court and census records for the name she gave me. Even though I knew I was born in Arkansas, I had no luck finding her. One day I was venting my frustration to a friend, and she told me her cousin, who was also an adoptee, had gone through a comparable situation to mine but was finally able to locate her birth family. She offered to check with her friend and obtain more information if I wanted, and of course, I said yes. Hearing back from her the next day, she gave me the name of an adoption service in Little Rock, Arkansas, and explained that social workers at the agency helped adoptees locate their birth families. After legally obtaining the original birth certificate, a social worker conducted a search for the birth parents. If birth relatives were located, the social worker telephoned them, explained the situation, and asked if they would permit the adoptee to contact them. If they agreed, the social worker gave the adoptee the name and phone number of the relative and it was necessary for the adoptee to pursue personal contact, if they desired.

"Immediately after receiving this information from my friend, I contacted the agency and went through all the necessary steps: filling out, signing, and returning paperwork, and sending the required fee for their service. Finally, weeks later, I received a phone call from the social worker. Holding my breath while waiting for her news, I was ecstatic when she told me she had found my birth mother, who agreed for me to contact her. Summoning all my inner strength, I made the phone call. A woman answered and identified herself as my mother. The sound of her voice overwhelmed me with emotion, and when I identified myself, she was equally as emotional. I told her the reason I was contacting her, and she agreed to meet me in person and supply me with all the family's medical information, plus If I was interested, she would explain the circumstances which had occurred, forcing her to place me in an orphanage.

The following weekend, we travelled to the town in Arkansas where she was currently living and met her for lunch. To finally meet the person who gave birth to you face to face was very awkward, along with being emotionally challenging. On one hand, I felt somewhat of a kinship to her and caught myself trying to find physical features we both shared, but at the same time, I felt guilty for having positive feelings towards a person who gave me away. We shared a lengthy conversation, with her explaining the circumstances which forced her to place me for adoption.

"My mother told me I was born when she was young and that my birth father was in prison at the time. If all the details she shared were not emotional enough, she then topped it off by telling me I also have three sisters. When his sentence was up, my parents eventually reunited and had three more daughters. She said my sisters were now waiting at her house to meet me if I was willing to follow her there. Chuck looked at me, and I nodded my head *yes* in agreement.

Meeting my sisters face-to-face turned out to be both terrifying and exciting at the same time. We talked for hours, trying to catch up on years of likes and dislikes, and finally ended up with promises of staying connected with each other, which we have done. Sadly, though, I learned the breast cancer gene was present in our genetic makeup, and I was not the only one in my birth family fighting cancer.

Sandy's heartwarming story had us all mesmerized, and an air of melancholy settled around the table. After everyone had composed themselves, Sandy looked at me and said, "I would love to hear you story also, Margaret, if you wouldn't mind sharing it."

We ordered our entrees, and as we were waiting for them, I briefly told them the circumstances surrounding my adoption, starting with the skeleton I found in the drawer. I knew Sandy would completely understand the frustration, sorrow, and anger I 've been feeling all these years so, when I finished my story, I wasn't surprised to see tears running down her cheeks.

She said, "I'm so sorry you had to go through the trauma of making this discovery on your own. I can't even imagine what that must have felt like. Margaret, if you are interested, I can contact the social worker in Arkansas that helped me and see if there is a similar agency in Mississippi."

Jumping up from the table, I hugged her and said, "Absolutely, I would love that!" Finally receiving our entrees, we changed the conversation from the intense content to lighter subjects. We finally ended our meal with cups of weak Texas coffee and left the restaurant just before closing time.

K.C. and I were supposed to return home early the next morning but Sandy, hoping to contact her social worker to obtain the name of an agency in Mississippi, asked us to stay longer, if possible. We took our time packing our belongings while Sandy was working in her home office, and then we followed Chuck to one of his barns to K.C. a couple of new fillies that had just been born.

Suddenly, I heard Sandy shouting, "Margaret, I got the name of the agency for you. It's in Jackson, Mississippi."

Running out of the barn, I met her halfway in the yard, gave her a hug, and said, "I will never be able to thank you enough, and I pray this may finally be the key I have been looking for to free the skeleton from that drawer."

Of course, with all the commotion, K.C and Chuck hurried out of the barn, with Chuck asking, "Sandy, what in the world is going on?"

She told K.C. and Chuck the good news and they were as equally excited as we were. Finally saying our goodbyes, I hugged Sandy again, promised to pray that her cancer treatment would be successful since she now had her genetic information, and promised to keep them informed about the results of my search.

It's difficult to explain the mixture of feelings I experienced after our visit. I was grateful for Sandy's help, sad was sad to hear the news of her cancer, ecstatic at the prospect of another possible search method to obtain my birth information, was worried the search would prove to be another dead end, and scared scared the agency might find members of my birth family who would decline to have contact with me. On our return trip home, I discussed the pros and cons of each situation with K.C. and he believed it was worth the risk and encouraged me to follow through with this new lead.

I still couldn't help wondering *Am I strong enough to manage all the possible risks of searching again?* The past twenty years of my life, getting on and off that roller coaster, had been exhausting. There were "ups" of fear and anticipation when I had new search leads, but each time, the experience just ended with "downs" of disappointment. Between the "ups" and "downs" I felt as if I was existing in a never-ending line, just waiting for the next roller coaster to come along. Now I saw another ride approaching, and I found myself facing the dilemma of whether I would board it again for one final ride.

CHAPTER 25

Roller-Coaster Finale

Christmas music was playing on our radio's FM station, as I sat on the floor in our den, wrapping last minute presents. I was oblivious to the music, being deep in thought as to whether I was going to contact the agency in Jackson, Mississippi. For an unknown reason, a popular Christmas song playing on the radio interrupted my thoughts. I suddenly found myself sharing the melancholy feeling evoked by the artist who was singing about missing a loved one and and having a blue Christmas without them. I tried to finish wrapping the gifts, but a little voice in the back of my head kept interrupting my concentration. *Why do I have to continue missing someone special in my life? I have another chance to finally find Diane, free that skeleton, and end this nightmare. The lyrics of the song may be a sign I should try one last time. What more could I stand to lose?* Since it was still early afternoon, I got up from the floor to find the phone number Sandy had given me and I carried it, along with the telephone with the long extension cord back into the den. Before I could change my mind, I quickly made the fateful phone call to the agency in Jackson. Impatiently waiting for someone to answer I sat gazing into the fireplace, hypnotized by the flickering of the flames. A female voice finally answered, and was asking repeatedly, 'Hello, hello, is anyone there?' Her voice breaking my trance, I apologized, and I said, "'I'm so sorry, I guess my mind just wandered off.'"

Very sweetly, the young lady asked, "How may we be of service to you?"

Nervously clearing my throat, I replied, "A friend of mine, who is an adoptee, gave me the name and phone number of your agency. For health reasons, she needed to find her birth mother to obtain her genetic medical history. She discovered an agency in Arkansas, where a social worker helped her by successfully finding her birth mother. As a favor to me Sandy called her social worker to inquire if Mississippi had an agency such as the one in Arkansas, and the social worker gave her the name and address of your agency. I was born and adopted in 1943 through a private adoption and informed years later that I had an older birth sister, who I have been unsuccessfully looking for."

Finally completing my long reply, the young lady said, "I am so sorry, Ma'am, but I will have to transfer you to one of our social workers. Would you mind holding, please?"

Frustrated at my rambling on to the wrong person, I answered as politely as possible, "Not at all," and said a silent prayer for courage and patience.

In just a couple of minutes, a more mature voice answered and said, "Hello, my name is Janice Hollingsworth, and I am one of the social workers at our agency. Please just call me Janice, as I like to keep our interactions on a more personal level. And to whom do I have the pleasure of speaking with?"

I gave her my name, and she said, "Margaret, please tell me the reason you have contacted our agency."

Trying to briefly explain my situation, I repeated what I had just told the receptionist. Janice said, "Well, Margaret, you have indeed contacted the correct agency. Let me start by asking the mandatory questions and we can continue from there. First, I'm sure by now you are familiar with the Mississippi law that requires the sealing of all adoptees' birth certificates unless there is a written release by the birth mother attached?"

I said, "Yes, I went through another agency in Biloxi years ago to fulfill the counseling requirements for a social worker to conduct a search for my birth certificate. About a week later, she obtained it and sadly informed me that my birth mother had not attached a letter of release."

Janice continued, "Then let me explain the difference between our agency and the first one you contacted in Gulfport. Our goal is to try to reunite adoptees with their birth families, but only after determining if the birth family is agreeable to having contact with the adoptee. We start by obtaining a copy of your original birth certificate, conduct research on the names of your parents, and, if we find a living relative, we contact that person, explain the situation, and ask if they would be agreeable for you to call them. If they are, we give you their name and phone number, and it is your responsibility to pursue any further connection with them. If your relatives decline any contact, I'm afraid there would be nothing further we could do. There are hourly fees connected with our search, as well as transportation expenses, documents to complete, and a contract, which you must agree to sign. I know I've covered quite a bit of information in a brief period, so please let me know if you have any questions about our procedure which I may not have covered, Margaret."

Since this process was exactly what Sandy told me she had gone through, I couldn't think of any other questions, so I said, "None that comes to mind right at the moment, Janice."

She continued, "Do you agree with the terms, or do you feel you need more time to think about it?"

Without hesitation, I replied, "I totally agree with the terms."

She then began a general question-and-answer session, telling me she may need to contact me later for more information, and finally asked me to give her the details about my search efforts.

I began by re-telling the details of my first contact with the agency in Gulfport, the census searches conducted by me and K.C., and about the private investigator I hired.

Janice said, "Margaret, I think there is a good chance I will be able to help you, but I must warn you there is always a possibility of negative discoveries, or refusal by the birth family for you to contact them."

I replied, "I understand the outcome is not guaranteed to be a positive one, but I believe I am emotionally ready to accept whatever results you find."

She said, "Okay, then I will place the necessary paperwork in overnight mail to you. As soon as I receive the completed forms and fees from you, I will begin."

After informing her that I would also return the fee and completed documents by overnight mail, Janice continued, "I promise to do everything in my power to find your sister, and before Christmas, if possible. I believe if that were to happen, and she agreed for you to contact her, it would give each of you a special reason to celebrate the miracle of birth that this holiday stands for."

Tears welling up in my eyes, I said, "Janice, you have no idea what it would mean to me to finally be able to put this family skeleton to rest. And if you could pull off the miracle of finding Diane by Christmas, I would be forever grateful."

Hanging up the telephone and bursting with excitement to share my news, I looked out the back door and saw K.C. at the barn with the farrier. Knowing they would be busy for quite a while, I decided to call Mama.

When she answered the phone, and heard the excitement in my voice, she said, "Come on, tell me! It sounds like you have good news."

"Well, Mama," I said, "I have quite a lot to share with you."

Giving her a recap of our visit to Sandy and Chuck's, I concluded by saying, "And a Christmas song gave me the sign I needed to try one last time."

Laughing, Mama said, "What are you talking about, Margaret? How could a Christmas song have given you a sign about what to do?"

When I finished explaining my experience she said, "Well, you know Baby, I have been saying a lot of novenas, and maybe that was the sign I have been praying for."

"Mama," I said, "I hope and pray you are right, but I can't help feeling scared that we might just be in for a big disappointment once again. I called the agency in Jackson this afternoon and spoke with a social worker named Janice Hollingsworth. She explained the procedure, I agreed to the terms, so she is sending the paperwork by overnight mail for me to complete and sign."

Mama said, "It sounds scary for you to have to be the one to call your possible birth relatives."

I replied, "Yes, I can't imagine how terrified I will be if she finds someone and I have to call them, but since this is my last hope, I really don't have much of a choice." Hearing K.C. coming in the back door, I told Mama, "Let me run, I just heard K.C. coming in and I want to share the news with him. I promise I'll let you know as soon as I hear anything. I love you!"

K.C. took off his boots and walked into the den. Backing himself up to the fireplace to thaw out, he asked me about my afternoon.

I said, "Well, I finally got an answer about my search dilemma from a Christmas song I happened to hear on the radio while I was wrapping presents."

He replied, "Would you please explain how a Christmas song could possibly have anything to do with finding your sister?"

Starting to walk toward the kitchen, I said, "I'll fill you in after I get us something warm to drink. Coffee or hot chocolate?"

He responded, "I think I'll have a cup of hot chocolate for a change, and it might help if you put a shot of brandy in it so I can prepare myself for the story you are about to tell me. Are you sure you haven't been nipping on the brandy yourself?"

Laughing, I said, "No, I have not.

Returning to the den minutes later with our drinks, I sat down on the ottoman closest to the fireplace, handed K.C. his mug of hot chocolate, tipped my cup against his and said, "Here's to Christmas songs and their words of wisdom."

K.C., shaking his head in confusion, said, "OK, let me hear this story."

I retold the story of wrapping presents, with Christmas music playing over the FM Christmas station, and my mind being miles away, when suddenly a song with melancholy lyrics about having a blue Christmas without a loved one, abruptly returned me to the present. I started listening to the lyrics and it was as if it was telling me that I might not have any more Christmases without Diane if I pursued the lead Sandy had given me. I know this sounds bizarre, so I called Mama and told her about my experience. She didn't seem to think it was unusual at all, since she has been saying novenas to give me a sign which would lead me to my sister, whom she is convinced is not dead. She believes this song may be the sign.

K.C., laughing, looked at me and said, "Well, I'm not sure a Christmas song was telling you what to do, but I definitely agree with your mother that you should pursue the lead Sandy gave you."

I said, "Thanks, I'm glad that's how you feel, because I already called the agency!"

He jumped up, gave me a bear hug, and said, "I'm so proud of you for taking that step, my love."

After we settled down, I told him everything Janice had explained to me about the procedure, and that now it was just a matter of time waiting for the papers to arrive.

As Janice had promised, I received the Priority Mail Express overnight packet from her agency the following day. I sat down at once, completed the forms, signed the contract, enclosed my check, and drove to the post office that same afternoon to mail it back to her by overnight delivery.

Struggling to be patient, I practiced my yoga relaxation techniques, and somehow managed to survive the next couple of days. Each time the phone rang, I felt my heart jump into my throat from excitement and dread. Finally, on the third day, which happened to be the day before Christmas Eve, I was again sitting on the floor, wrapping one last-minute gift when the phone rang.

Feeling my heart in my throat and my stomach doing flip-flops, I ran to answer it and heard a familiar female voice say, "Margaret, this is Janice. Are you able to talk now?"

Almost breathless, I answered, "Yes, of course."

"Okay," she continued, "I have uncovered two contacts in my search, which could lead to finding your sister. Are you ready to listen to my entire report?"

Feeling dread, as I detected concern in her voice, my mind sped ahead, imagining all the possible worst-case scenarios she could give me.

Trying my best to calm down, I asked Janice if she would please hold the line for a minute, and she said, "Of course, Margaret."

Setting the phone down, I focused on my breathing to keep myself from hyperventilating. When I finally felt in control of myself, I picked up the telephone receiver and said, "I guess I'm as ready as I'll ever be, Janice, but somehow I have the feeling you aren't going to give me good news."

She said, "You are astute, Margaret, but I have questionable news, good news, and unfortunately, sad news. Would you like to get a pen and paper so you can write down the information I'm going to share with you?"

Excusing myself to find a pencil with a decent point and a notepad, I returned to the phone and said, "I'm back, but I'm not sure if I will be able to decipher my notes since my hands are shaking so much."

She laughed, then continued, "Margaret, let me begin with the unwelcome news on your birth mother's side of the family. I'm deeply sorry to say that I was unable to discover any clues which might lead to locating Diane, nor your birth mother. Either one of them could have different last names due to re-marriages once or twice, and divorces as well. The good news, however, is I did find a male relative of Mayme's who lives in Arizona. I spoke with him and, and since he is not a direct relative, I only told him you were trying to find Mayme, but I didn't disclose the fact that she is your birth mother. He admitted he was related to her but was not comfortable sharing any further information with me. He agreed, however, to speak directly with the person who was trying to contact her. Are you ready to write down his name and phone number?"

Responding, "I'm ready," with my hands shaking uncontrollably, I wrote the information on the notepad as clearly as I could.

Janice continued, "Now, Margaret, let me tell you about the paternal side of your birth family. The sad news is, I was able to confirm the fact that your birth father died years ago. The good news, however, is that I called and spoke with his widow, who shared very surprising information with me. Your father married her a couple of years after your birth mother placed you for adoption, and they had seven children together during their marriage."

There was a pause in the conversation as Janice waited for my reaction. Trying to wrap my head around this shocking news, I was unable to find any words to express what I was feeling. All I could say was, "Wow! I certainly never expected to find out I had more siblings. You have no idea how strange it feels to have started off as an only child, then to discover I have a sister, and now for you to be inform me that I have seven siblings on my birth father's side of the family.

She responded, "Margaret, I can't begin to imagine how you must be feeling right now. But, let me warn you again. Don't get your hopes up by thinking any of your birth family will welcome you with open arms. Your father's widow did say she is willing for you to call her and will answer any questions you might have about your birth father, his medical history, as well as what she knows of his ancestry. Now, try your best to write down her name and phone number so you can read it after we hang up," she laughingly told me.

When I was able to complete this simple task, I read my scribbling back to her and she verified it was correct. Janice finally said, "Unfortunately, that is all the information I was able to discover, Margaret. I wish you the best of luck in the continuance of your search, and I pray for a Christmas miracle in finding more information on Diane or Mayme from the male relative I spoke with. Please call me or send a note to let me know how everything turns out for you."

Thanking her profusely and wishing her the merriest of Christmases, I promised to stay in touch with her.

After hanging up the phone, I sat stunned, trying to process what Janice had just shared with me. There was so much information spinning around in my head, I had trouble trying to focus on just one issue at a time. And the thought of calling and talking to people who were my blood relatives, but at the same time total strangers, had me terrified and physically sick to my stomach. *How would I start off the conversation? What would their reactions be, and how would I react to them? Would I receive the information I needed to finally find Diane, or would I find out it was another dead end, or the report that she had died in a plane crash was indeed true?* Trying my best to stop the incessant questions bombarding me, I walked outside in the chilly air, partially to try and clear my head, but also looking for K.C. so I could share the information Janice had just given me. Finally spotting him in the distance, riding one of his client's horses in the outdoor arena, I decided to go back inside.

CHAPTER 26

Maternal Discoveries

Walking back into the kitchen, I brewed a pot of coffee and sat down at the table, looking at the two names I had written on the notepad, my mind drifting, trying to imagine the variety of paths our conversations could take. When the coffee had finished brewing, I poured myself a cup and sat down in the den near the fireplace, watching the flames dance around the logs. Just as I had finished my cup of coffee, I heard K.C. come in the back door. I knew the smell of the freshly brewed coffee would stop him in his tracks and seduce him into pouring himself a cup of the steaming liquid. I called out, "I'm in the den."

Walking in with his coffee cup in hand, he took one look at me and sat down on the hearth. He said, "You talked to the social worker, didn't you? Your face is beaming."

Jumping up and throwing my arms around him, I said, "Yes! But along with exciting news, there are questionable leads and of course, dead ends. I can't wait to tell you the details of the overwhelming conversation I just had with Janice."

Having warmed himself enough from the direct heat of the fireplace, K.C. settled down in his recliner, and I curled up on the couch. I started at the beginning of my conversation with her and told him word for word every detail she had shared with me.

He stopped me mid-sentence when I got to the part about having seven siblings on my birth father's side of the family, and exclaimed, "Wait a minute! You are telling me that you have seven more siblings? At the rate of growth in your family, we will go broke trying to buy gifts for everyone at Christmas."

I gave him one of my *seriously?* looks, as he grinned and apologized. "I'm sorry, I was just trying to lighten up the intensity of the conversation."

Thanking him for trying to be helpful, I continued with the rest of the details, concluding with my fear and dread of having to call those people.

He said, "Sweetie, after all you've been through for so many years, I'm totally convinced you are up to the task of making those two phone calls."

Sitting in silence for what seemed like hours, I jumped up and said, "You are right! I can, and I am going to do it right now!"

He got up, gave me an encouraging hug, and said, "I'm so proud of you."

Blowing him a kiss, I retreated into the office, closed the door, said a prayer, took meaningful breaths, and dialed the number of Dennis Woodard, the male relative of my birth mother.

The infernal ringing of the telephone when you're anxiously waiting for someone to answer it can be maddening. Finally, after what seemed like an hour, a man with a rapid Yankee clip to his friendly-sounding voice, entirely foreign to the southern accents I grew up hearing, answered the phone. Hesitating, I was unable to admit the true reason for my call, even though I had rehearsed the conversation over and over in my head beforehand. Instead, I impulsively made up a story and gave him a fictitious name instead of my real one.

Beginning the conversation formally I said, "Mr. Woodard, my name is Elizabeth Babin. A social worker from an agency I hired to search for Mayme Woodard, a lady whom my mother has been trying to locate for years, gave me your name and phone number as someone who may be able to help me. My mother worked with Ms. Woodard years ago and they became quite close friends. Since my mother is getting up in age and has something of a personal nature belonging to Mayme, she would love to be able to return it to her, in person, if possible. The social worker was not able to locate Mayme but told me she had found a male relative of hers. After speaking with you and getting your permission for me to call, she phoned me and gave me your telephone number." Pausing, I took a deep breath, and waited for his response.

It felt as if my whole lifetime was floating past me in slow motion as I waited for his reply. Dennis finally said, "That's right, I did give the social worker permission for you to call. I'm Dennis, Mayme's younger brother, but unfortunately, my sister is having serious health issues right now and isn't physically able to talk with you, even if I were to give you her telephone number. She is living in Las Vegas with her husband, and I think it would best if I give you her daughter Diane's phone number, and suggest you contact her. She will be able to fill you in on the details of Mayme's condition, and most importantly, if she would agree for your mother to visit her."

There are absolutely no words that could come close to describing the feeling I had at that moment. I wanted to scream out, *Diane is alive!*

I was doing my best to stop the room from spinning, and obviously it took me quite a while to ground myself, because Dennis interrupted my state of frenzy by repeatedly asking, "Hello? Hello? Elizabeth, are you still there?"

Coming back down-to-earth I finally said, "Yes, I'm so sorry. Someone just walked into the room to ask me a question."

He continued, "No problem. Would you like for me to give you Diane's phone number?"

I answered, "Oh, yes, please. I would appreciate it very much."

Once again, I found myself trying to write down another name and phone number with shaky hands, but this time it was the name of the person I had been trying to find since the day my mother told me I had a sister.

Diane's last name was not Mildon, which explained why I didn't have any luck initially searching for her. That was the last name of her first husband. After their divorce, she remarried, and now her last name was Hollowinski. I said, "I can't thank you enough, Mr. Woodard, for giving me this information, which I hope and pray will help me in Mama's search for her friend."

He said, in his quaint accent, "You're quite welcome, young lady."

Little did I know as I hung up the telephone, I would soon be meeting my Uncle Dennis in person.

Sitting silently in our office, tears running down my cheeks, I felt so overwhelmed by the news my uncle had just revealed to me that I had trouble breathing. Trying to prevent myself from hyperventilating, I focused on deep breathing until I finally felt able to stand up, but still weak-kneed, I slowly walked into the den to share this staggering news with K.C.

When he saw my face, he turned off the TV and asked, "Are you all right? You look as pale as if you have just discovered another skeleton." Quickly walking over to take my arm and guide me to the sofa, he continued, "What happened? Do you want me to get a cold rag for your face?"

Saying, "No thank you.", I sat speechless for what seemed like hours, rather than minutes. After trying to find words that would even come close to describe how I was feeling, I finally said, "The male relative I just called instructed me to call his niece, Diane, if I wanted further information about her mother. Do you realize what that means? Diane is very much alive!"

My body, filled with adrenaline from the revelation I had just received, was unable to sit still. I suddenly jumped up, grabbed K.C., and we hugged and spun around the den like a couple of kids. Finally getting dizzy, we sat down on the sofa, and he said, "I'm so excited for you, my love. This is just unbelievable! I want you to start at the very beginning of your conversation with the man you called and tell me every single word."

Catching my breath, I said, "First of all, the man I spoke with just happens to be Mayme's younger brother, Dennis. He told me, with a very quaint accent, I might add, that if I wanted information about Mayme I would have to contact her daughter, Diane, because his sister was in failing health and would not be able to communicate with me. He said Mayme was still living at home with her husband, but Diane is helping with her mother's daily needs. So, then he asked, 'Would you like me to give you Diane's phone number?' I thought *Seriously, I have been waiting for her telephone number for years!* Of course, I could not tell him that, but I politely and as calmly as possible said, "Yes sir, I would appreciate it very much.'"

K.C., who had been anxiously waiting for me to finish sharing the story, said, "Well, what are you waiting? Go call your sister!"

CHAPTER 27

The Reality of a Dream Come True

If I thought the other telephone calls, I had made during the years of my search had been difficult, not one of them came even remotely close in comparison to the ultimate one I was now ready to make. I walked into our office, lied down on the day bed trying to relax, focusing on the Christmas music I could hear softly playing through the closed door to the office, and the scent of the cranberry-cinnamon candle wafting in from the dining room. I knew this meant K.C. had opted for music and his crossword puzzles, rather than turning the television back on. Allowing myself to relax and practice my yoga breathing, I finally felt a little calmer and more in control of my emotions. I reached for the phone, which rested on one of the side tables next to the day bed, stared at it, and realized that whatever I was getting ready to hear over this instrument would change my life forever.

Finally dialing the phone number Uncle Dennis had given me, my heart pounded with each unanswered ring. After what seemed an eternity, I heard a woman's deep voice, with a similar accent to that of Uncle Dennis,' say, "Hello."

Struggling to find my voice, I managed to utter the words, "May I please speak with Diane Hollowinski?" Waiting breathlessly for her reply I experienced a weird, otherworldly feeling, as if I were floating on a cloud, looking down on this drama from above.

The deep voice on the other end of the phone brought me back to reality when she replied, "This is she."

Once again, I lost my courage to begin with the real reason I was calling, so I used the same fabricated story I had told Uncle Dennis. I said, "I'm trying to find Mayme Mildon, who was a friend of my mother's when they worked together at the Markham Hotel in Gulfport, Mississippi years ago. Now that my mother is getting up in age, she would love to see Mayme in person, if possible, to return something of a personal nature that belongs to her. I have been conducting searches on my mother's behalf for years, and a friend referred me to an agency who was able to locate Mayme's brother. I phoned him, and he gave me your telephone number, saying you would be in a better position to help me."

Pausing to catch my breath, Diane shocked me by interrupting with an unrelated question. "When is your birthday?" she asked.

Not sure why this was important enough to be the first thing she asked me, I hesitantly told her my birth date, and she responded with a tearful voice filled with emotion "You're my sister, Margaret, aren't you?"

It's impossible to explain the feelings coursing through my veins at that moment. Reconnecting with my sister had finally extracted the skeleton from that drawer, buried it forever, and in the process had reattached a missing piece of myself.

Struggling to find my voice, I managed to weakly utter, "Yes, this is Margaret. Are you really my sister, Diane?"

She started crying and said, "Yes, I am, and you have no idea how many years I've been searching for you."

If this had not been such a dramatic moment, our conversation would have seemed comical. Each of us had so much information we wanted to share and so many questions we wanted to ask, that we found ourselves jumping around from one subject to another, often talking at the same time, with one of us constantly saying, "I'm sorry, you go ahead."

I said, "Diane, one of the first things I want to share with you is an ironic piece of information I received from a private detective I hired to find you, and which almost caused me to discontinue my search. He told me he located an article about a plane crash years ago, which was responsible for the death of a young girl named Diane, along with the pilot, whose last name was the same as Mayme's. I almost called off my search after receiving this tragic news, but my adoptive mother and my husband kept nudging me to continue searching. I finally learned of an agency that uses social workers to search for family of adoptees. After paying their fee and supplying what little information I had, they reported they could not find my birth mother but had found a male relative of hers, and he agreed for me to contact him. She also reported that my birth father was deceased and gave me the number of his widow. You cannot imagine the emotional shock I felt when I called this male relative, making up a story about my mother searching for Mayme, and he told me I would need to call Mayme's daughter, Diane, to get more information."

Diane responded, "I think I can imagine how you felt, because I wasn't sure if you were dead or alive either. I know it will take the rest of our lives to catch up on all the years we've been apart, but first, Margaret, there are three important things I want to share with you now. But before I begin, would you please give me a couple of minutes to explain to my husband what's going on? You see, he is deaf, and being unable to hear my side of the conversation, is upset because he sees me crying and is scared that something is wrong. Let me tell him who I'm talking to and assure him these are tears of joy."

"Of course, Diane," I said. "Please take your time explaining what's going on."

She placed the phone down, and as I was waiting; I could hear her voicing the words as she was obviously signing them, and then I heard her husband's deep chuckles, mixed with the sound of crying.

Diane picked up the phone again and said, "Okay, I'm back. My husband's name is Clarence, but everyone calls him Chummy. He tearfully said for me to tell you hello and how happy he is about us finally finding each other."

I said, "I'm so sorry about his disability, Diane."

Thanking me, she said, "He's been deaf since childhood, is well-adjusted, and has been able to maintain a job as a sheet-rock specialist." We talked about Chummy, his handicap, and how it had affected their family. She said she learned sign language when they started dating and their two sons learned to sign as they were growing up, so they were all able to communicate with one another. Changing the subject, she said, "Let me get back to the three things I want to tell you before we go any further."

"First, our mother is still alive, although she is suffering from Alzheimer's disease and is not doing well mentally. She is still currently living at home with her husband, Bob, but he is unable to totally care for her. I go to their house every day and bring them food, take care of the house, and help with her personal needs. I'm not sure how much longer we will be able to continue this arrangement because her condition is worsening by the day. Even though Bob is not in favor of putting her in a professional facility, I'm afraid we will soon have no other choice. Margaret, if you have any desire to meet our mother, you really should try to arrange a trip to Las Vegas as soon as possible; but I must warn you that even if you do decide to come, and we visit her, she won't remember you, even if I tell you who you are. There are days she doesn't even remember me, Chummy, or the boys."

"The second thing I want you to know is that I only found out I had a sister when I was a teenager. When Mother and I moved back to Michigan from Mississippi we were living with my great-grandmother, grandmother, and Uncle Dennis. One day, a cousin of mine, who derived immense pleasure from bullying me, got angry, and blurted out, 'Diane, you're so clueless, you don't even know you have a little sister somewhere.'"

Of course, I was shocked, but thought surely, she was just making up a story. I fretted over her accusation, and finally decided to confront Mother. On one of her rare days off from work, I saw her sitting alone on our front porch steps, reading a book. Walking out of the house, I sat down on the step next to her and said, "Mother, I have an important question I want to ask you."

Putting her book down in her lap, she said, "Okay, Diane, what is it?"

With a tremble in my voice, I asked, "Do I have a younger sister I don't know about?" I turned to look at her, saw her face turn pale, and a look of pain and sadness filled her eyes. I sat, holding my breath, waiting for an answer.

She finally said, "Yes, Margaret you do have a half-sister, but the details are too painful for me to talk about. I can only tell you I had no choice but to give her up for adoption when she was three months old. I have no idea of her whereabouts, and I cannot even remember the name of the family who adopted her. Now, Diane, I have answered your question and I don't want you to ever bring up the subject of your sister again."

I walked back into the house, went to my bedroom, and lied down on my bed, trying my best to grasp the story Mother had just revealed to me. Suddenly, I had an idea how I might be able to get more information. Our Uncle Dennis, who I always called "Unc" was living at home when I was in Gulfport with Mother. I thought he must be aware of the adoption, so I decided I was going to ask him. That night I waited until I knew everyone was sleeping. Quietly slipping down the hall, I tapped lightly on his door and whispered just loud enough for him to hear me, "Unc, can I come in? I have something important I must ask you."

He answered, "What is so important that you must talk about it in the middle of the night, Diane? Can't it wait until morning?"

I replied, 'No, it's about a secret Mother just told me and it has me really upset."

"Okay, he said, come on in."

When I entered his room, he was sitting up in his bed, so I sat down on the foot of the bed. As I tentatively sat there, he asked, "Okay, Diane, what is this secret?"

Hesitantly, I asked him, "Unc, do you know if I have a sister who was given up for adoption"

The shocked expression on his face was answer enough, but I still wanted to hear him say the words. He finally replied, "I'm sorry, Diane, but I'm afraid it's sadly true. One day, about a year after Mayme moved to Gulfport, I happened to overhear a telephone conversation between Mother and Mayme. I was shocked when I heard Mother say, 'Mayme, you and Diane are welcome to return home, but there is no way you are going to bring *that baby* with you.' I was shocked, not only because I wasn't aware that Mayme was having another baby, but also because I couldn't believe our mother would not allow her to bring your sister home. I will remember those words for the rest of my life."

Diane continued, "After the conversation I had with Unc, I started searching for you. I did manage to get a copy of your adoption papers from the Clerk of Courts office in Mississippi, which gave me the names of your adoptive parents, but unfortunately the document didn't supply any useful information, such as the state where they were from. I searched as much as possible in Mississippi, but obviously I didn't have any luck finding your adoptive parents there.

The third thing I want to share with you is our mother's love life. Mayme was an attractive and popular woman who loved to dance and party and who always had a boyfriend throughout high school, and right after graduation she married my father. After I was born, their marriage started falling apart, and she finally forced him to leave our great-grandmother's house. Over the years, our mother married five more times, each relationship being tragic and abusive. I had five different stepfathers growing up, and none of them, except her current husband, proved worthy of her. Margaret, it's obvious that fate did not bless our mother with having good judgment in men. The strangest thing of all, however, is despite the five marriages, she never had any other children. Now that I have filled you in on the most vital information, I wanted to share with you, do you have any other questions you would like to ask me, Margaret?"

Uncle Dennis and Diane had both revealed the most shocking fact that my birth mother was still alive, as well as Diane sharing other stunning facts with me, so I was unable to think of anything else to ask her.

I said, "No, Diane, none that I can think of right now. My head is reeling from everything you just shared with me."

We continued to talk, however, for at least another hour, trying to catch up on a lifetime of stories, exchanging momentous events and laughing and crying at each other's stories. Before we hung up, Diane promised she would make copies of the pictures of our immediate family members she kept in her family album and label each one so I would have the opportunity to see my current and deceased family members. She said she would either give it to me in person if we were able to arrange a trip to Las Vegas or mail it to me if we were unable to go.

Diane's compassionate and considerate offer touched me profoundly, and I found myself in tears once again.

After thanking her, I said, "Let me think about coming, Diane. I have mixed feelings about meeting our mother, but I can hardly wait to meet you in person. I'll talk to K.C. and Mama, get their input, and see if, and when, we could arrange a trip."

She said, "I totally understand if you prefer not to meet our mother in person, Margaret."

I replied, "Thanks for understanding, Diane. I'll let you know what I decide to do and will keep you updated."

Both of us were choking back tears as we finally agreed to say, *we'll talk soon*, instead of saying *goodbye*.

After that emotional conversation, I again felt the need of solitude in our office to stretch out on the day bed and process the information my sister had just given me. The words *my sister* felt foreign, even in my thoughts. Taking the next step, I said the words *my sister* aloud over and over. Vocalizing and hearing them seemed even stranger. Again, turning my attention to the sound of the beautiful carols on our CD player, I realized miraculous circumstances had given me the most special Christmas gift I had ever received, and my Christmas would be anything but blue this year.

Abruptly, my thoughts turned toward Mama. I knew she would be overjoyed when she heard this news, but since it was getting late and Mama went to bed early each evening, I decided I would wait until the next day to tell her about the incredible news in person. Besides, in my heart I knew I wanted to share this ultimate experience with K.C. first.

Filled with emotion, I walked into the den, and the comforting warmth and aroma of the oak logs burning in the fireplace welcomed me. K.C., who had been sitting in his recliner listening to Christmas music and working on a crossword puzzle as I had suspected, got up when he saw me and asked, "Are you okay? You look exhausted."

After I collapsed into my chair, I answered, "I do feel physically and mentally exhausted, as if I just completed a marathon. It's hard to understand that receiving exhilarating news could leave someone feeling so emotionally drained."

K.C. said, "Just relax, and give yourself time to sort through all the information your relatives have provided you with today. I'll be back shortly."

Hypnotized by the warmth of the open fire, the soothing sound of the Christmas carols, the smell of the Christmas tree and the delightful odor of the cranberry-cinnamon candle burning in the dining room, I finally started to relax and realized I would now be able to trace my ancestry and would no longer be tormented by the skeleton in that drawer.

K.C. walked back into the room later, having given me enough time to sort through everything I had been through that day. I could smell the aroma of cinnamon wafting from the mugs of warm eggnog he carried with him. Thanking him, I sipped the comforting liquid and asked if he was ready to hear my story.

"What do you think? I've been waiting anxiously for you to get off the telephone," he laughed.

"I'm sorry for not telling you when we hung up, but it was just so overwhelming I needed time to process all the information. Obviously, I did talk to my sister for quite a long time, as you are aware."

K.C. started grinning when I said *my sister* and said, "I love hearing you say that. Sorry for interrupting. Go ahead, I'm listening."

I started with my reaction to the strange question she asked me when I first called. I told him about her finding out about me, and the fact that she also failed in her search. I told him about our mother, Diane's family, and finally finished by telling him of the debilitating disease our mother was suffering from. "You know, K.C., I have always been curious about learning my genetic identity for a couple of reasons. One, being able to discover my ancestry, and secondly to obtain medical information. Now, having knowledge that my birth mother has Alzheimer's I'm having second guesses about being aware of this."

K.C. answered. "It's important for you to know your medical history and be able to inform your doctors in order for them to monitor you for any symptoms of Alzheimer's, which could result in immediate treatment."

Nodding my head yes, I said, "I know you're right, but it's still scary."

Finally, I told him about Diane making me a duplicate family picture album, and her invitation for us to go Las Vegas so we could meet each other in person, and depending upon how soon we could travel, the possibility of meeting my mother if she were still alive. Diane did tell me, however, that she doubted Mayme would remember anything about me, as there were days when she didn't even communicate with, nor recognize her.

As I paused to take another sip of my eggnog, K.C. responded, "Well, when are we going to Las Vegas?"

I laughed and responded, "I was waiting to see if you agreed, which you obviously do. I would love to go as soon as we are able to arrange our schedules. However, I'm still not sure if I want to meet my birth mother."

K.C. got up, took my mug, put it on the mantel, hugged me, and said, "I can't wait to meet your sister. I'm sure she will love you as much as I do."

CHAPTER 28

Paternal Discoveries

Having finished dinner, I looked at the clock on the mantel and decided it wasn't too late to make the final phone call. I told K.C., "I'm anxious to get this whole ordeal over with, so I think I'm going to call my birth father's widow right now."

He said, "I totally understand, Sweetie. Good luck. I hope this conversation goes smoothly and successfully for you as well."

Giving him a hug for good luck, I walked into our office. Only this time I didn't hesitate before calling because I didn't feel as emotionally invested in the outcome of the conversation with my stepmother. I reached for the phone, dialed the number, and while it was ringing, I thought, *Saying I have a stepmother sounds as foreign to my ears as calling Diane my sister, since neither of these words have been part of my vocabulary until now.*

A lady answered "Hello," in a crisp voice.

I said, "I'd like to speak with Virginia Belluga."

She replied, "This is she."

I suddenly wondered if she had been aware of my existence before Janice's phone call, but it became quite clear she had been because her next comment was, "Margaret, I was not surprised to hear from that social worker. I have always known about you, and I felt in my heart we would hear from you one day. I'm just surprised it took this long. But, before we continue our conversation, I want you to be aware that your birth father died years ago in a tragic accident."

Although slightly taken aback by this abrupt and unexpected greeting, I wondered how to respond. When she finally paused to take a breath, I said, "Yes, Ma'am, the social worker informed me that he died quite a long time ago. I'm deeply sorry for your loss. The reason I was searching for my birth father, Ms. Belluga, was not necessarily to interact with him, nor to become a part of his life, but only to obtain medical history from the paternal side of my family. It's been very frustrating for me over the years to answer questions about any pre-existing medical conditions with, 'I don't know, I'm adopted.'"

Pausing, I took a deep breath, wondering what to expect next, but her voice seemed warmer and more relaxed when she replied, "I'll be happy to provide you with the medical background I am aware of on your father's side of the family. But first, Margaret, would you like me to tell you what details I know about your birth mother and father's tragic love relationship?"

Shocked at the fact that she was bringing this information into our conversation, I hesitated before replying, "Yes, please, I would appreciate your sharing any background information with me." I heard her take a deep breath, and she began her story.

"Well, Margaret, I met your father about a year after he returned from World War II. We started dating and were married the following year. He didn't keep his past relationship with Mayme, and the fact that she had carried his baby, a secret from me. He even told me they had picked out the name Margaret for their baby if it was a girl. When he returned to Gulfport after his time overseas, his intention was to marry your mother. He was shocked when he learned she no longer lived in Gulfport, frustrated at not being able to get a forwarding address from her employer nor from the post office, and was heartbroken when he learned your mother had legally allowed another family to adopt you before she left town. Totally devastated, he tried everything he could think of to find you and your mother, even contacting old friends and acquaintances, but was unable to obtain any information. He knew there was no use trying to contact Mayme's family because he was aware of their disapproval of him. One day he ran into a young lady who had worked at the hotel with your adopted mother and she informed him that she had received a letter from Mayme after she left Gulfport and would be happy to share the return address with him. By the time he received this information and contacted Mayme, however, she informed him she had already re-married. There was nothing left for him to do but resign himself to the heartbreaking fact that the war had caused two more casualties, both in his personal life.

"He finally moved back home to Michigan, where we met about a year later, started dating, got married, and had eight children. One of them, a boy, died as a baby, but we were fortunate enough to have three more boys and four girls. Each time one of our girls were born, however, your father asked if we could name her Margaret. I'm ashamed to admit, however, that I refused each time. I was afraid if he heard your name constantly it might have caused him too many painful memories. I also feared he may have unintentionally shown favoritism to that daughter.

After excusing herself to get a drink of water, due to a coughing episode, I waited patiently for her to return to the phone. Minutes later, Virginia again apologized and continued, "Where was I? Oh, yes! I was telling you why I didn't want to name any of our girls Margaret. You see, your father and I never mentioned your existence to any of our children. So, when the social worker contacted me this morning, and asked my permission for you to call, I panicked, worrying that you had also obtained their contact information and may have called one of them first. Since your existence was a skeleton, which we had kept hidden in our closet all those years, I felt as though I should be the one to reveal your existence. Even though it was in the middle of the day, and they were all at work, I still felt the need to warn them. Not surprisingly, they weren't sure how they felt about the shocking news or if they wanted any part of having you in their lives." As she paused, my mind pictured a hidden skeleton in another family, only this time it had been hiding in a closet, not in a drawer.

Interrupting her at this point, I said, "Let me assure you, Ms. Belluga, I have no intention of contacting anyone in your family nor causing disruptions in their lives. If any of them decide they would like to reach out to me, I will leave my contact information with you and would love to hear from them; otherwise, as I said earlier, the main reason for contacting you is to obtain medical information from the paternal side of my family."

Replying, she said, "Margaret, please call me Virginia. And of course, I'll be happy to share the medical background on Lonnie's side of the family." As she told me of my father's and other paternal family members' medical conditions, I felt as though she was looking into a crystal ball and revealing my own medical history. The feeling of sharing a genetic kinship with someone, was a new experience for me since I shared hardly any of the same medical issues with Mama and Honey, since of course, we didn't share the same DNA.

Virginia then asked, "Do you need more time to write down all the information I'm giving you?"

I said, "No thanks, I'm keeping up by using Gregg shorthand, which I learned in high school."

Finally, she asked, "Is there any other information you would like for me to share with you?"

I responded, "Yes, if you don't mind. I heard from someone on my birth mother's side of the family that one of my father's sisters had travelled to Gulfport to help my mother care for me and my half-sister when I was born. Do you happen to know anything about that?"

I could sense her hesitation before she answered, "Yes, I do. Your father's youngest sister, named Shirley, did travel to Gulfport to help take care of you and your sister. She's still living, so I also called her after I heard from the social worker. I felt she would want to be aware of this unexpected news, and naturally, she was quite stunned. Years ago, your father mentioned the arrangement of Shirley trying to help him and Mayme with the children, but I never questioned him about the details. Unfortunately, when I talked to Shirley, she told me she was not sure if she wanted to be in contact with you. She said she was scared to revisit those memories because they might prove to be too painful for her. She did ask me, however, to get your mailing address, and when she was over the initial shock of this news, and thinking more clearly about the situation, she might write to you."

I sat silently for minutes and then said, "Virginia, I'm beyond grateful for your sharing the obviously painful memories of my birth mother and father's tragic love story and for providing the medical background information on my birth father's side of the family. If you have a pencil, I will be happy to give you my contact information."

She said, "Hold on for a minute, please, let me locate one." Returning, sounding out of breath, she said, "Okay, I finally found one. Go ahead."

I spelled my last name and gave her my address and phone number. After she had finished writing down the information, she repeated everything back to me to check for accuracy.

Not finding anything to further discuss with her I said, "Virginia, thank you again for speaking with me and providing me with parts of myself I was unaware of before we talked. And please be assured, I will not bother you or your children again."

Saying our goodbyes, we hung up, and I assumed that was the end of starting a relationship with any of my siblings on the paternal side of my family.

As emotionally exhausted as I was, I didn't feel ready to share this latest information with K.C. and Mama just yet. Sitting in silence and thinking back over the conversation with Virginia, I realized I was now experiencing new feelings. I became aware of the feeling of rejection the social workers had forewarned me about, and it was not a comforting feeling. To think of my birth mother allowing another couple to adopt me, even though there were extenuating circumstances, and then to eventually find genetically related family members who also wanted no contact with me, was devastating. Oddly, however, I also found myself feeling empathy for my half-siblings who learned the shocking news of a skeleton in their family the way they did, as I knew firsthand the turmoil of feelings they were now going through. Hearing the tragic story of my birth parents' fateful love affair left me feeling melancholy. I couldn't help but wonder how differently my life might have turned out if my father had returned to Gulfport before my mother found a family to adopt me. On the other hand, I also felt proud of myself for persevering in my search and discovering another piece of my ancestry, as well as my paternal medical history.

Returning to the present, I decided to find K.C., have a glass of wine in front of our fireplace, and share this latest information with him. I didn't want to tell Mama the details I had recently uncovered by telephone, so I decided I would share everything with her tomorrow, when we picked her up for Christmas Eve Midnight Mass.

Walking into the den, I found K.C. entranced by one of his crime shows on television, but he instantly hit the pause button when he saw me walk in, and asked, "Are you ready to talk about your last phone call? If so, I'll finish watching the end of this program later."

As I lowered myself onto the floor pillow in front of the fireplace, next to Sadie, one of our rescue cats, I responded, "I think so, but I'd like a glass of wine first."

Getting out of his recliner, he said, "On my way!" He returned with a glass and a bottle of Chardonnay for me. "In case you want more than one glass," he said, smiling, while holding a frosted mug of dark beer for himself. He poured my glass of wine and settled down on the hearth next to Sadie and me. Taking a couple sips of my Chardonnay, while staring at the flickering flames in the fireplace and listening to the purring of Sadie as I petted her, I finally felt peace and closure, as I realized I had reached the end of an extremely long and frustrating journey. The only scary thing I had left to conquer on the emotional roller coaster I had been on was to meet my sister face-to-face for the first time.

Breaking out of my hypnotic spell, I looked at K.C. as he patiently waited for me to start talking. Finally, I said, "Well, are you ready for another long story?" He nodded yes as he took a deep swallow of his beer.

I began. "K.C., you will never believe the first words my father's widow uttered after I said hello! She said, 'I knew we would hear from you one day.'" After repeating as much of our conversation as I could remember, I turned to the shorthand notes I had brought with me from the office for reminders of the things I may have forgotten to mention. As I glanced over my notes, K.C. went to the kitchen for another beer and I poured myself a second glass of wine. When he returned, I shared more details I had forgotten earlier, and said, "Well, that sums up our conversation."

He looked at me and the only thing he was able to say was, "Wow! I'm at a loss for words."

I said, "Don't feel all alone."

As a melancholy mood hung over the two of us, he finally added, "I'm sorry for the pain I know you must be feeling, but all I can say is, it's their loss for missing out on the opportunity to have you in their lives."

Giving him a hug for those sweet words, I said, "Thanks, I appreciate that." We sat in silence, finishing our drinks, and thinking about the dramatic scenarios that had played out today.

Feeling a growling in my stomach, I said, "I'm getting hungry. Let's get a bite to eat and go to bed early because I'm exhausted, and tomorrow is going to be another emotional day. I decided I would like to go to Mama's a little earlier tomorrow afternoon so I can share the latest search results and discoveries with her in person before we leave for Midnight Mass. I'm especially anxious to tell her the news about Diane."

K.C. said, "That sounds perfect."

CHAPTER 29

Christmas Eve

After pouring my morning coffee, I walked into our sunroom, sat down in one of the comfortable wicker chairs, propped my feet up on the ottoman, and gazed out at our tree-lined backyard as a squirrel scurried around, searching for acorns hidden among the leaves. I could hear the horses whinnying at the barn and knew K.C. was giving them their morning feed. I thought about all the new pieces of information I had discovered about myself. Although finding Diane was the ultimate reward, there was also the hurtful realization that I felt rejected once again, this time not by my mother, but by my father's family. Overall, I decided, the effort of struggling with my feelings and the frustrating search over the past years still had been worth the effort. Voicing my thoughts aloud to Sadie, who had jumped on my lap and curled up to take a nap, I said, "Yes, Sadie, it is indeed a special Christmas Eve."

Encouraging her to jump down and take her nap elsewhere, I got up and called Mama. When she answered, I said, "Merry Christmas Eve!" After our usual chit-chat, I asked, "Will it be okay if we pick you up a little earlier for Mass this afternoon?" I knew she was going to worry about something being wrong, so I added, "Don't worry, Mama. Nothing is wrong. I just have added information I want to share with you, but I would prefer doing it in person."

She replied, "Sure, Baby, I'll be ready early, and I'm praying this means you have some good news."

I said, "Well, let me just say it's mixed news, but I'm not going to tell you anything else right now. We'll see you later."

After having a late breakfast, we dressed and left for Mama's. As we arrived at her apartment, I found myself apprehensive about telling her the news I had received from Virginia. Mama was now in her mid-eighties and was living in an assisted living facility. Although she was still in possession of her mental faculties and could physically navigate with only the aid of a cane, she was still frail. When she opened the door and we hugged, I could feel her bony shoulders through the blazer she was wearing. I prayed this news would not put too much physical or emotional stress on her. K.C. also hugged Mama, and he and I sat down on the sofa in her small living room. Mama, of course, sat down in the same platform rocker she had moved twice during her life. Once we were all seated, Mama asked her usual question, "Would y'all like coffee first?"

I looked at K.C., he shook his head *no*, and I wasn't in the mood either, so I said, "Not now, Mama, maybe we'll have some if there is time after I update you on our recent discoveries."

She settled back in her chair, slowly and easily rocking it back and forth, and said, "Okay, Margaret, I'm ready. Please tell me what you found."

"Well, Mama, the social worker, Shirley, called me yesterday and told me she had no luck finding Diane, but she was able to give me the name and phone number of a male relative of Mayme's, who agreed to give me information if I called him. She was also able to verify the information given to me by Mr. Duke that my birth father was deceased, but she gave me the telephone number of his widow, Virginia, who agreed to share information with me if I called her."

Looking at Mama, I noticed she was sitting up on the edge of her chair, nervously wringing her hands in her lap. She finally said, "For goodness' sake, Margaret, will you please tell me if you found Diane?"

I replied, "I'm getting there, Mama. As you used to tell me all the time, 'Just hold your horses!'"

She couldn't help but laugh, and at least that helped her relax a little. Once I saw her settling back into her chair, I continued my story.

"So, Mama, I called Mayme's relative first, who turned out to be her younger brother, Dennis. I didn't tell him who I was because I panicked at the last minute, but I felt sure if he knew his sister had felt adoption was the best choice for her baby, he must have suspected my identity. Anyway, I ended up telling him I was trying to find Mayme for you because y'all had worked together during the war, and you had something personal of hers you wanted to return in person if possible. And guess what he told me, Mama?"

She said, "I have no idea, Margaret Ann, but if you don't hurry up and tell me I'm going to scream."

Laughing, I continued. He told me if I wanted information about Mayme, I would need to contact her daughter, Diane. Obviously, I was in total shock and unable to find words to answer him. When I finally found my voice, I told him I would appreciate it very much if he would share her contact information with me.

He gave me her last name, spelling it, since it sounded Polish, her telephone number, and address, which happens to be in Las Vegas. Saying our goodbyes, I thanked him for his help, and before I could lose my courage, I called the number he gave me."

Giving Mama time to let this much of the shocking news settle in, I saw she was struggling to get out of her chair. K.C. and I both rushed over to help her stand up, and she hugged each of us and cried in our arms. "Baby, I can't begin to tell you how happy I am for you," she said. "This is the best Christmas present I've ever received. Now, please go on and give me all the details of the conversation between you and Diane."

Helping her to sit back down in the platform rocker, K.C. and I took our seats, and I continued my story.

"Mama, it was so strange, because when I called Diane, I lost my courage again and started off the conversation in the same way I had with our uncle. However, her first words were, 'When is your birthday?' I told her, and she replied, 'You're my sister, Margaret, aren't you?'"

"I can't begin to tell you the shock I felt when she dropped that bombshell on me. I again found myself speechless. Finally, I tearfully said, 'Yes, I am.' All we could manage to do for what seemed like hours after that was cry and talk over the top of each other.'"

I continued telling Mama all the details Diane had shared with me and ended up by sharing the news that Mayme was still alive but was suffering from Alzheimer's disease.

Mama interrupted by saying, "Oh, Baby, I'm so sorry to hear that."

I said, "Diane told me if I have any interest in seeing her in person, I should arrange a meeting very soon, as she is declining rapidly."

Now, let me tell you about the other phone call I made to my birth father's widow, Virginia. When she answered the phone, and as soon as I said hello, she said, 'I know you are Margaret, and I was afraid we would hear from you one day. Unfortunately, you won't be able to have contact with your father because he died in a tragic accident. We had eight children together, with one dying as a baby, and none of our children were aware of your existence until I called them today.'"

I looked over at Mama, and saw she was getting pale, struggling to absorb all the information I had just given her. I asked her if she wanted me to continue, and she said, "Of course, I do. I'm perfectly capable of handling anything else you tell me." Smiling to myself, I finished telling her the rest of the information Virginia had shared with me.

The three of us sat quietly until Mama broke the silence. She said, "Margaret, I have one more request of you. Besides meeting

Diane in person, I also would love for you to have the opportunity to meet Mayme before she dies."

Tears started rolling down my cheeks as I looked at this woman, I would always consider my mother, with love and admiration for showing me what unconditional love was all about. Standing up, I lifted her out of the chair, and again we cried and hugged. I said, "Mama, I will think about it, but right now it's time for us to leave for church. We'll discuss this later."

She picked up her purse and cane, while K.C. picked up her overnight suitcase, since she was going to spend the night with us after Midnight Mass. That way she would be with us for our traditional Christmas at K.C.'s parents' house next door to the ranch. K.C. opened the door for us, and as Mama took my arm she said, "Just so you know ahead of time, Margaret Ann, if you decide to go to Las Vegas to see Diane and Mayme, I plan on going too."

As K.C. closed the door behind the three of us, all I could think of replying to this shocking and unexpected statement was, "We'll see, Mama."

CHAPTER 30

A Christmas Surprise

Upon arrival at the ranch after St. Joseph Cathedral's Midnight Mass in Baton Rouge, I was still humming the carols K.C. and I had sung with our magnificent choir, accompanied by the organist's beautiful strains on the Reuter's Grand Pipe Organ. As I was preparing the drip coffee pot for later in the morning, after we would hopefully get at least a couple of hours of sleep, I noticed the flashing red light on the answering machine in the kitchen.

I hit the play button to listen to the message as I poured myself a glass of water and froze when I heard an unfamiliar male voice say, "Welcome to the Belluga family, Sis. This is your brother, Bill. I grew up thinking I was the eldest of the seven of us, but I just found out yesterday that I have an older sister. Please call me when you have time to talk, because we have quite a bit of catching up to do. I wish you a Merry Christmas!"

I replayed the message over and over, because hearing someone else addressing me as "Sis" was strange, but at the same time also heartwarming. It was too late to return my brother's call, and besides, my head was still spinning from trying to wrap itself around all the information I had received over the last couple of days. I got ready for bed, but filled with so many new emotions, and as exhausted as

I was, I had trouble going to sleep. The conversations with my uncle, my sister, my stepmother, Mama, and the phone message from my brother kept playing over and over in my head, bringing with them droves of new feelings. I eventually drifted off to sleep, but instead of visions of sugarplums dancing in my head on this Christmas Day, I had visions of faceless new relatives, and images of what they might look like.

Waking up later that morning, I could smell the aroma of fresh coffee, so I put on my robe and slippers, passed by the guest bedroom to check on Mama, and since she was still sleeping, I shut her door. I made my way to the kitchen to help myself to a cup of the steaming liquid, walked into the den, and was met by twinkling lights on our beautiful seven-foot Scottish Pine Christmas tree, and by the crackling fire in the fireplace, which K.C. had prepared ahead of time. I sat on one of the floor pillows with my back to the fire and stared at the angel perched atop the tree. I felt that this special holiday, celebrating the birth of Jesus, was a proper time for me to also celebrate my own birth story, which I had finally discovered. As I sat musing the recent events, I remembered the strange sensation I felt when I heard the melancholy words of the Christmas song the other day and thought to myself *This is certainly not going to be a blue Christmas.*

The sound of the back door closing interrupted my thoughts, as I heard K.C. humming a Christmas carol when he walked into the den. I stood up, hugged him, and said, "Thank you so much for having the coffee made, a warm fire started, and for lighting the Christmas tree. But most importantly, I want to thank you for the love and support you've given me while I kept boarding and un-boarding that nerve-wracking roller-coaster all these years."

He said, "Believe me, my love, just seeing the look on your face yesterday after you talked to your sister made it all worthwhile."

Although I was thoroughly enjoying the comfort and bliss of this special time with K.C., I reluctantly got up, saying, "I would love to stay right here all day, and I would like to call my brother back, but I'm afraid I don't have enough time to get involved in a lengthy conversation. I need to get busy making the potato salad and pecan pie for our Christmas meal."

It had been a tradition for years to have a late Christmas lunch, or early supper, depending on the time of day all the relatives arrived at K.C.'s parents' house. In addition to his family: a sister, brother, four nieces and two nephews, K. C.'s family always included Mama, my Godson, whom we had practically raised from a small child, his wife, and two children.

K.C.'s dad, who I always called Pop, prepared the turkey, his mother made a delicious cornbread and oyster dressing, and the other adults supplied side dishes and desserts. We were indeed fortunate to indulge in such a delicious feast.

K.C.'s mother, who I called Mom, always decorated their house to perfection, as she was very artistically talented. She always put up two Christmas trees, a formal one inside the living room, where we opened our gifts, and a whimsical one in the large glassed-in sunroom, where we ate our delicious meal on a quite large table for the adults and several smaller ones for the youngsters, who were able to enjoy watching the toy train travelling beneath the tree. She also had Christmas villages placed in four rooms of the house and a beautiful crèche adorning the mantel in the living room. The family, usually dressed in Christmas-themed outfits, arrived bearing food and gifts and greeted each other with hugs and kisses. The adults scurried around setting tables, warming prepared dishes, and placing pitchers of iced tea, water, soft drinks, along with bottles of wine on the sideboard.

Before everyone sat down to dinner, Pop called everyone to encircle the main table, holding each other's hands. After leading us in a Christmas blessing, he invited each of us to add a prayer or request if we wished. As he was praying, the blessings I had to be thankful for this year overwhelmed me. I found myself not only praying for my adoptive parents, but now realizing the tough decisions made by my birth parents when I was born, I found myself praying for them as well. When it was my turn to voice a special intention, I took a deep breath and said, "I recently discovered some wonderful news, and I would like to share it with y'all. I feel sure everyone here is aware that this wonderful lady next to me that I proudly call Mama, and my loving father whom I called Honey adopted me as a baby. After discovering years later that I also have a maternal half-sister, I began a search for her. A Christmas miracle happened this year, because not only did I find her, but we talked to each other on the telephone yesterday."

It was all I could do to hold back a flood of tears, but as I looked around, I saw that other family members were shedding tears of their own. After the prayers and petitions, everyone gave me congratulatory hugs and asked endless questions. Eventually we made our way to the tables and enjoyed our boundless feast of turkey, dressing, and all the fixings.

After returning home later that afternoon, I summoned enough courage to return my brother's phone call. When he answered and I said, "This is Margaret," he sounded genuinely happy to hear from me.

He replied, "I'm so grateful you returned my call, Sis. We have so many years to catch up on, I'm not even sure where to begin. Why don't you begin by telling me about yourself, and how you were able to locate us after all these years?"

Smiling and thinking to myself I had found another relative who talked as fast as I did, I said, "It's a long story, little brother, are you sure you want to hear all the details now?"

He chuckled and said, "It sounds strange hearing you call me little brother, since I grew up believing I was the oldest sibling in our family. Sorry for interrupting, but it's amazing to learn I have an older sister."

I said, "I completely understand. Can you imagine how I felt when I discovered I not only have a half-sister on my birth mother's side of the family, but in searching for her, I discovered I have four half-sisters and three half-brothers on my father's side of the family? It was beyond overwhelming!"

After we exchanged laughs, I briefly told him the story of my search. He then shared humorous and melancholy stories about our father: his personality, occupation, talents, likes, and dislikes. It felt strange to learn that I shared so many of my father's interests and personality traits. Bill then continued by telling me about each of our siblings and their families, and said, "Margaret, for the life of me I can't figure out why any of our siblings would have a problem with you contacting them. More importantly, I can't understand why Aunt Shirley feels it would be too painful for you to contact her. Obviously, since I didn't know about you until my mother called yesterday, I have no knowledge of the circumstances surrounding the time she cared for you as a baby."

Thanking him, I said, "I appreciate your kind words, Bill, but I am sure each of them will need to deal with the skeleton that just fell out of your family's closet in their own way. Please tell me about your own family."

He responded by telling me about his three sons from two different marriages, and added, "My oldest son, Ryan, lives in Tucson, Arizona and is a senior in college there. If you ever find yourself travelling out West, please stop by and meet him. He is a fine young man who plans to enter medical school as soon as he has completed his senior year of undergraduate studies. I called him last night and told him about you, and he said he would love to meet his new aunt."

I said, "As a matter of fact, I'm planning to take a trip to Nevada as soon as possible to meet my maternal half-sister and my birth mother, who is in the final stages of Alzheimer's disease. If possible, I would love to stop by and meet my nephew on our return trip."

Bill responded, "Wow, that sounds like a trip you can't afford to pass up!"

We talked a while longer, promising to stay in touch with each other, and planning to set up an arrangement for the two of us to meet in person as soon as possible, somewhere between Pennsylvania, where he lived, and Louisiana.

I received another surprise a couple of days later, when I received a telephone call from Uncle Dennis. When I answered, he said, "Margaret, this is your Uncle Dennis, Unc, as everyone calls me." He started chuckling, a sound which seemed to originate from deep in his belly and resonated somewhere in his throat, causing his laugh to come out sounding like *yucks*. It was unique, and it was a sound which put a smile on my face.

He continued by asking me, "Are you able to talk right now? If so, I would be happy to share everything I know about your adoption."

I said, "I'm so happy to hear from you, Unc, and yes, I have time right now, and would very much appreciate your help in providing more of the puzzle pieces surrounding my adoption."

He said, "I suspected it was you who called me right before Christmas looking for Mayme, but I thought it should be up to Diane to share the information you were looking for. I have known about your existence since Mayme called home from Gulfport when you were just a baby to beg our great-grandmother to allow her to return home and of course, bring you and Diane with her. I happened to be in the room when she received the phone call; and I heard our great-grandmother say, 'Mayme, you can come back home and bring Diane with you, but not *that baby*.' It broke my heart to know she would have no other choice, if she returned home, but to place you with someone for adoption.'"

Hearing this story firsthand by someone who had overheard the conversation, confirmed the story Mayme told Mama years ago before my adoption. Suddenly overcome with sadness and compassion, I couldn't imagine the pain, torment, and betrayal Mayme must have felt when her mother gave her that ultimatum.

Responding to his comment, I said, "Unc, I know it was devastating for Mayme, but it must have also been traumatic for you, and must have affected your life as well. You have no idea how appreciative I am for your telephone call, and how meaningful it is to me that you shared that experience with me.

He answered, "You're right, Margaret. That phone call did set a new course for our lives, and I appreciate your being empathetic about my situation." We continued chatting about our families and exchanging a lifetime of stories. I found myself totally intrigued by his jovial personality and distinct laughter as I listened to him as he shared amusing memories.

I finally said, "Unc, it's getting late, I'm emotionally exhausted, and I'm sure you must be too. I think we should continue sharing our lifetimes of memories another day."

He replied, "I agree, Margaret, but I have one request to make. If you decide to travel to Nevada to meet Diane, and possibly Mayme, please let me know. I would love to travel to Diane's house at the same time so I can also meet you in person." Touched by his request, I said, "I promise, Unc, to keep you informed of our travel plans. I would love to meet you as well."

CHAPTER 31

Travel Plans

Deciding to take the advice of K.C., Mama, and Diane, I started planning the trip to Nevada. Of course, the primary reason for going was to finally meet my sister, but I was also anxious to meet her husband, Chummy, their two sons, Mark, and Kevin, and of course, Unc. Although I'm not sure if I would have taken the trip just to meet my birth mother, I had to admit I was curious about having the opportunity to see her face-to-face, even though I was aware she wouldn't have any idea who I was. That would be a blessing for each of us, as it would be less emotional, and by meeting her, I felt I would finally be able to banish every remnant of the skeleton I had found in that drawer, for the last time. I was also looking forward to meeting my paternal nephew, Ryan, on the return trip through Arizona, if we were able to work the visit into our travel itinerary.

The first item, and the most difficult, on the checklist I had made for planning our trip, was for us to be able to coordinate finding workers who could run K.C.'s horse business, and for me to find a reputable sitter for our inside pets. Luckily for me, I was off during the summer, a benefit of working in the school system, so arranging my dates for the trip was not difficult. When K.C. and I were finally able to find and schedule the employees we needed, I called Diane with the dates, and she assured me they would work perfectly for her and her family.

The next phone call I made was to Unc to be sure the dates would be convenient for him. He said, "As I mentioned before, Margaret, I'm retired, so almost any dates would work for me, and those are perfect. I can't begin to tell you what it would mean to finally meet Mayme's youngest daughter."

I replied, "I assure you, Unc, I'm just as excited to meet you. I'll keep you informed of the exact day we will be arriving and where we will be staying."

The next item on my checklist was a little more difficult. K.C. and I preferred to fly rather than endure a three-day road trip each way. Mama, however, being adamant about going to Nevada with us, insisted she would not fly. Other than her fear of running out of necessities, she suffered from other fears as well. One of them, sad to say, was a fear of heights, which naturally explained why she refused to fly. After taking college courses in psychology, I came to understand that often people's fears are the result of having endured a traumatic experience in their lives, which had been out of their control at the time. My grandparents raised Mama during the recession following World War 1, and she had no control over the economic challenges which her family faced and caused them to struggle for years. Fearing that she might face that trauma again, she became extremely frugal, holding on to anything she felt might be remotely reusable. I believe that flying, which was also out of her control, stirred up other insecurities, such as her fear of heights. Although I tried my best to reason with her about the advantages and safety of flying, I finally had to accept the fact that I couldn't change her mind. Knowing this trip meant so much to her, I was not able to bring myself myself to go without her. After talking it over with K.C. to be sure the barn help would be able to work the extra time we would have to spend on the road, which luckily, they were, and the pet sitter would also be available, we finally agreed to drive the 3,200-mile round trip by car.

I called Mama, and said, "Guess what, Mama? You can start planning a long road trip to Las Vegas." I gave her the dates, which were about a month away.

She said, "Baby, thank you so much for doing this for me. I'm so excited, and I can't begin to tell you how happy y'all have made this old lady."

I found myself having to add another item to my checklist. Since we were now driving, I wanted to travel in a vehicle which would supply maximum comfort for Mama. K.C. and I discussed this dilemma and knew we certainly couldn't take the trip in my compact economy car and obviously, not in K.C.'s pickup truck. So, I started calling rental agencies to price luxury rental cars and the cost to rent a vehicle for that length of time was shocking. When K.C.'s parents discovered the dilemma we were facing, Pop called and asked us to drop by their house that afternoon.

Of course, we agreed, and as we sat around talking about our trip, Pop said, "Mom and I have figured out a solution to your transportation problem. We insist the three of you take our Lincoln Continental. It will supply a smooth and comfortable ride, and Margaret, it will allow your mother enough room in the back seat to lie down and take a nap when she gets tired."

Stunned by their offer, I said, "You're both so generous, and I sincerely appreciate your kindness, but I wouldn't feel comfortable borrowing your car for the extended time we'll be gone."

Just like his son, Pop was very stubborn and wouldn't take no for an answer. I realized we finally had no other choice but to accept his offer, so I told them, "I thank you both from the bottom of my heart, and I promise I will never forget your generosity."

With the major plans finally in place, the final item on my checklist was to decide on the location of our first meeting with Diane and her family when we arrived in Las Vegas. We had discussed this on the telephone, and she said, "Margaret, you know you, K.C. and your mother are welcome to stay at our house. It's not large, but I can certainly find enough places for each of you to sleep."

I said, "I appreciate the offer, Sis, but I feel as if this would not only be an inconvenience, but I think we might all be more comfortable if we stayed at a hotel or a condominium. Teasing her I continued, "You never know, we might not like each other after we meet face-to-face."

She started laughing along with me, and said, "I seriously doubt that would happen, but you're probably right about all of us feeling more comfortable if our first meeting took place on a neutral site."

Besides, I continued, "Since K.C. has never been to Las Vegas, and Mama and I haven't been since they moved the old strip years ago, I thought we may as well take advantage of this opportunity to do a little sightseeing while we're there, so I'm thinking about making reservations at the Flamingo Hotel. A couple of my friends recommended it and I also read complimentary reviews about it in various travel guides."

She responded, "That's an excellent choice. Not only is it in the middle of the New Strip, but it's also the oldest hotel on the New Strip. Famous celebrities have performed there over the years, and in fact, still do."

I said, "I'm glad you approve. I'll make reservations right away."

Diane said, "There is another issue I need to talk to you about, Margaret. I hope you understand it will be necessary for all of us to go to Mother's house for the first meeting. Leaving their house presents too many physical and emotional challenges for her. So, what if the three of you meet me, Chummy, our sons, and Unc, at our mother's house, the day after your arrival?"

I said, "That sounds perfect. Pausing to think about what she just said, I added, "Diane, I have to tell you how strange, but incredible it felt to hear you call her "our" mother." I heard her sniffling, so I asked, "Diane, are you crying?"

Sobbing now, she said, "You have no idea how grateful I am that you feel the same as I do. I need to apologize, however, since I become overly emotional at times."

Responding, I said, "You certainly don't have to apologize to me for feeling that way. We are both entitled to having intense feelings since we've been through so much, don't you think?"

She laughed and said, "You're absolutely right, little sis."

Sniffling, I said "And, finally, after the long journey we've travelled, it's hard to believe that I'm actually hearing you say those words."

We were both so excited about the upcoming reunion, we continued to talk, laugh, and cry for another hour.

In addition to the generosity already shown by K.C.'s parents, they insisted on helping us financially with our travel expenses as well because they wanted this momentous trip to be perfect for me, Mama, and Diane. We tried to turn down their offer but soon realized they weren't going to take no for an answer. Pop said, "Margaret, we want you to use this money to book a suite so there will be plenty of room for the three of you to sleep, as well as having a sitting area, which will give your family enough space in which to be comfortable when they visit you at the hotel."

Hugging them one at a time, I said, "Thank you both for your thoughtfulness. Loaning us your car was generous enough, but now to make our hotel stay luxurious, is beyond my wildest dreams. I will be forever grateful to both of you for making this trip so special."

So, when making reservations at The Flamingo Hotel and Casino, I checked the prices of the variety of suites which the hotel offered. I finally settled on a Metropolitan Suite, not one of the largest and most expensive, but one which was quite large, had two bedrooms, a Queen, and a King, plus a sitting area with a sectional sofa and a small dining area.

Finally, the day before our departure, I started going through my clothes to decide what to bring, and K.C. brought our suitcases down from the upstairs closet. As I folded my clothes and laid them out, along with my shoes, I looked at the open suitcases on the bed, and I suddenly started getting butterflies in my stomach. A fleeting thought of cancelling the whole trip entered my mind since the idea of meeting my birth mother in person and spending time with my sister and uncle was terrifying. *What if we all feel so awkward around each other the entire experience ends in a disaster?* I asked myself. Then the next minute, I found myself overcome with excitement at the thought of coming face-to-face with people who shared my genetic makeup. Despite the conflicting feelings, I knew I had to pursue this journey, which started so many years ago, and lay to rest the final remains of the skeleton I had found in that drawer.

Mama had stayed with us the night before we left, since we planned to leave early the following day and it would save us time by not having to travel miles out of the way to pick her up. Waking up the next morning after a fitful night of trying to sleep, I put the coffee on to drip and noticed Mama already sitting in the sunroom.

As I walked in, she said, "Baby, I can't tell you how delighted I am for you to have this chance to meet Diane. It's a dream come true for me, and I thank you and K.C. for allowing me to tag along."

Hugging her, I said, "I'm happy you are coming with us too, Mama. We just hope you will be comfortable, and the trip won't be too hard on you. Just let us know whenever you need to stop and walk around to stretch your legs. Excuse me for a minute. I'm going to check on K.C., and I'll bring you a cup of coffee when I come back."

I walked out the back door and saw him in the barn finishing the morning feeding. I called to him, "Coffee's on!" He raised his hand in acknowledgement and came inside minutes later. As he sat down in the sunroom with us, he asked, "Well ladies, are you ready for a road adventure?" We both responded, at the same time, "You bet!"

So, on an early June morning, with promise and excitement in the air, we packed the Lincoln Continental Mom and Pop had so generously loaned us. We were able to leave quite a bit of room for Mama, as well as a pillow and light throw cover on the back seat, and her sewing bag fit perfectly on the back floorboard. As we pulled out of the driveway, I took a deep breath. Everything was finally in place to start the most meaningful trip of my life, the one which would end with me finally meeting my sister and mother face-to-face. The thought of arriving at our destination brought feelings of anticipation, but with fear mixed in as well. I asked myself, *Will I be able to manage the rejection if Diane decides she doesn't like me or doesn't want me in her life after we meet? After everything that has happened to me in the past,* I thought, *I'm sure I am strong enough to survive any outcome.*

CHAPTER 32

An Unforgettable Side Trip

We decided, since we were taking this long road trip out West, we should take advantage of the opportunity to throw in a little sightseeing along the way. K.C. had never been farther west than New Mexico, so we thought it would be a perfect time for him to visit famous sites he had never seen. The Grand Canyon was on the top of the list, as well as a side trip to Sedona, Arizona, which had been highly recommended by friends, relatives, and tour companies. Honey, Mama, my cousin, Becky, and I had taken a trip out West when I was in high school to visit Honey's uncle in Arizona, but after he and my great aunt toured us around to see the Petrified Forest, Painted Desert, and Grand Canyon, we didn't have enough time to go to Sedona. After we left my great-uncle's house in Arizona, however, we did travel further west to Las Vegas just to see the lights of the casinos and hotels on The Strip. Years ago, however, the city built The Strip on Fremont Street, so now Mama and I were anxious to see the much larger and more elaborate New Strip, which was four miles long, and now located on South Las Vegas Boulevard.

The first day on the road was quite boring, as we drove through west Louisiana and over miles of the flat wide-open ranges of Texas, and finally stopped outside Amarillo for the night. It was a long drive, but Mama insisted she was fine, having taken naps during the day. When planning our trip, I made reservations for two nights in Sedona, so we could use one of the days for a trip to the Grand Canyon, which was just a couple of hours away.

When I had explained our travel plans to Mama before we left home, she said, "You two are welcome to go to the Grand Canyon, but I have no desire whatsoever to go back there again. The terrifying heights scared me to death. I'll be fine staying in the hotel and working on a baby blanket."

The side trip to Sedona turned out to be a harrowing experience for Mama, however, and one we weren't sure she would survive. Thinking I had everything perfectly mapped out before we left home, I failed to notice that the Oak Creek Canyon Road, running south from Flagstaff to Sedona, although only fourteen miles, had a dramatic elevation drop from 7,000 feet to 4,500 feet. The drive was on a winding, two-lane road, passing through ponderosa pine forests, buttes, switchbacks, and it eventually ended in the city of Sedona, dramatically surrounded by beautiful million+ year-old red rocks.

Mama, feeling terrified during the tedious and dangerous forty-five-minute drive, kept up a steady, anxiety-ridden moaning and groaning every time she tried to uncover her eyes and look out the window at the beautiful vista. After each futile attempt she would lie back down on the seat and repeat over and over, "*Y'all just had to go to Sedona!*"

Although the drive certainly was awe-inspiring, it was also tedious and presented a challenge in maneuvering the curves, especially in our Lincoln. Concerned Mama may end up having a full-blown panic attack or even worse, a heart attack, we did our best to keep her as calm as possible, constantly reminding her to lie down, close her eyes, and take deep breaths. We had no choice but to continue this route to Sedona, as there was no place to turn around safely, and by the time we reached the most tedious part of the drive, we were more than halfway there. With extremely skillful driving by K.C. we finally reached our destination, with Mama in good condition.

Once out of the car we stood mesmerized by the beauty of the Sedona Verde Valley surrounding us. Mama took a deep breath. and said, "Even though the drive was terrifying, I must say I'm glad I survived the nightmare just to see this magnificent sight."

When I booked our hotel reservations, the picture of our hotel, featured in the AAA Travel Guide, showed only the front, and it was on street level. I chose it for Mama's benefit, and to further ensure her comfort, I also requested a room on the lowest possible floor.

After checking in at the front desk we took an elevator to our room on the second floor. Opening the door and turning left to place our personal belonging on the dresser, we found ourselves facing floor-to-ceiling windows, revealing a breathtaking view of the surrounding valleys, interspersed with beautiful red rock formations and luscious evergreen vegetation. The perspective changed completely, however, when we walked right up to the window to get a closer look. Unfortunately, the picture I had seen in the travel guide was deceiving, as it didn't reveal the extreme height we faced when looking straight down from the window. Mama followed us to the window, looked down, turned white, quickly backed up, and said, *"Y'all just had to go to Sedona!"*

Trying not to laugh at her theatrics, we finally calmed her down and K.C. moved a chair as far away from the window as possible, and I brought her a bottle of cool mountain water, compliments of the hotel. After sitting there, sipping her water, she finally relaxed enough to pick up her sewing basket and focus on her baby blanket.

After bringing in the luggage I told Mama, "We're hungry, so we are going to take a walk down the street and get a bite to eat. Would you like to come with us or would you rather we bring you something back?

She said, "I'm tired, so I think I'll just stay here and take a hot bath. I would appreciate it, though, if y'all would bring me a sandwich or a cup of soup."

Closing the curtains, I said, "Mama, now you won't have to look out the window at all if you don't want to. We'll be back with your supper as soon as possible."

K.C. and I walked around town, enjoying the quaintness of the beautiful town, and the amazing beauty of the red-rocked mountains and valleys. We found a cute café, with outdoor seating, which advertised Elote Dip. When planning the trip, I remembered travel agencies recommending this specialty, as it was a favorite in Sedona. The dip is based on the flavors of South American street corn and consists of corn, mayonnaise, Cotija cheese, tortillas, and other spices. Entering the café, we each ordered a bowl to go, and since Mama's stomach is not able to tolerate spicy food, we ordered a cup of chicken soup and a side salad for her. We walked outside and sat at one of the tables, while waiting for our order, and were fortunate to watch the breathtaking sunset, another one of the wonders of Sedona.

When our order was ready, we walked back to the hotel, and the first thing we noticed when we entered the room was the fact that Mama had opened the curtains again, although her chair was still in the same place. She thanked us for her supper, and said, "I hope you two were able to see the beautiful sunset. It was stunning! And I want to assure you I'll be fine staying in the room alone tomorrow, if my chair and I don't get too close to the window."

Laughing along with her, we dove into our supper, and I agreed that the recommended Elote Dip had indeed lived up to its' reputation.

After we returned from an early breakfast the next morning, we got Mama settled in the room before we left for the Grand Canyon. I said, "Mama if you need anything, just call the front desk. We let them know we'll be gone all day, and they assured us they will look after you if you need anything. There is room service here, so when you get hungry, just press the button on the phone that says, "Room Service" and order whatever you want from the menu on your bedside table. And don't worry about paying. The hotel will automatically charge the meal to our room tab."

She responded, "Stop worrying so much, Baby. I'll be fine."

Giving her a kiss goodbye, I glanced back at her as we walked out the door and humorously noticed that she had scooted her chair a little closer to the window.

The side trip to the Grand Canyon was well worth the four-hour round-trip. The majestic beauty and massiveness of the canyon, which has taken almost two billion years for the Colorado River to carve out, overwhelmed K.C. and we found it difficult to pull ourselves away from one of the most spectacular wonders of the world, but we wanted to return to Sedona before dark. We left, however, with a promise of a return visit.

When checking out of the hotel the next morning, which happened to be a Sunday, I asked the hotel clerk for information on Catholic churches in the area. She said, "If you haven't already been there, you must go to the Chapel of the Holy Cross. It's nearby and is famous for its' magnificent view of the Mystic Hills surrounding it through the glass floor-to-ceiling windows behind the altar.

I said, "That sounds perfect! Thank you for the suggestion, and if you don't mind, please give me directions."

Returning to the car, I told Mama, "The manager recommended we go to this beautiful little chapel close to here for Mass, and as it turns out, we'll be able to get there in time for the nine o'clock service. It's just a short distance off the main road, but we'll have to drive up into the Mystic Hills to reach it. The manager assured us the road is very safe."

Mama said, "Okay, I'll do my best to stay calm. It can't be any worse than the road we took from Flagstaff to get here. If it gets too bad, I promise, I'll just close my eyes."

As we wound our way up, Mama was so focused on the chapel in the distance, which looked as if it was jutting out of a red rock wall, she barely paid attention to our drive. After arriving and parking our car, we made our way up the entrance ramp leading into the chapel. After walking through the door and turning left to face the altar, we stood transfixed as we stared at the magnificent ninety-foot-tall steel cross which was hanging behind the altar and seemed to be embedded in a huge red rock, the beauty of the Mystic Hills in the distance, and the entire breathtaking scene framed by floor-to-ceiling glass windows. We stood, staring in awe, before making our way to an empty pew. After Mass was over, we continued sitting in our pew, absorbing the beauty, and feeling an overwhelming sense of peace and tranquility.

As we walked out of the chapel Mama said, "I'm so grateful y'all took me here. It was one of the most moving experiences I've ever had. Now, if only we didn't have to return to Flagstaff on that scary, winding, cliff-hanging road!"

We had to laugh, although it really was an appropriate description. Her only omission was the fact that the return drive offered more awe-inspiring views of the beautiful red-rock valley in the distance.

I said, "Mama, we'll take our time driving back down. All I want you to do is either concentrate on your sewing or try lying down on the seat and saying a rosary."

As we slowly made our way down the mountain, Mama only looked up from her sewing a couple of times, gasped, put her head down, and emitted *Oh-Oh's*, but never once repeated the mantra she had continuously recited on the trip down into the valley.

CHAPTER 33

One Last Night on The Road

Since our reservations at the hotel in Las Vegas didn't start until the following night, we intentionally planned to stop one more night on the road, closer to The Flamingo, so we would be able to arrive early in the afternoon, allowing time for our visit with Diane, Chummy, and Unc.

After we safely returned to the flat stretch of the interstate, we stopped in Flagstaff for lunch and then continued west to Seligman, Arizona. Since K.C. and I had always been fans of the TV series, *Route 66*, I planned our next stop for a night in this small, historical town, situated about an hour west of Flagstaff. Seligman is known as the birthplace of Historic Route 66, named by Angel Delgadillo, a barber, who opened his shop there in 1950. The other seven states through which Route 66 passed, formed their own Route 66 associations, and a worldwide, nonprofit organization dedicated to the preservation of Route 66, founded the National Historic Route 66 Federation. We arrived in town early enough to settle into a room at the original, but renovated, Route 66 Motel. It was very quaint, as I remembered stopping at motels like this one when Honey, Mama, Becky, and I had travelled out West.

After we settled in our room and washed up, we decided to have dinner at the also famous Roadkill Café, which I had researched before leaving home, and had read great reviews about. Although the food was tasty, the best part of the experience was reading the names of the entrees on the menu such as Fender-Tenders, Splatter Platter, Highway Hash, and Swirl of Squirrel, among others. After dinner, we walked over to the Historic Seligman Sundries Building. To show the age of this historical building, built in 1904, the owners had a bright yellow 1972 Ford Ranchero parked outside in front of the store. As we walked in, the first thing that caught our attention was a vintage soda fountain in the middle of the store. We walked around for a while, checking out the Route 66 souvenirs and memorabilia from Elvis and other famous celebrities who had visited the establishment. We picked out souvenirs to bring to our friends back home and visited the vintage car and motorcycle museum, found in the rear of the store. By the time we had finished with our shopping and sight-seeing, we decided we would feast on ice cream from the soda fountain for dessert.

Getting tired, we made our way back to our motel. We turned on the TV to catch the news and took turns taking baths. Settling in our beds, K.C. asked me, "Are you ready to finally meet your sister tomorrow?"

I responded tentatively, "I am, but I must admit I will get little or no sleep tonight since I cannot seem to stop the fluttering of butterflies in my stomach. The feeling I have right now is like the feeling of expectation mixed with fear I get when the cable on a roller coaster builds up a supply of potential energy and pulls its' riders slowly up that first steep hill of a roller coaster. I am just hoping and praying that tomorrow I will feel nothing but the sheer exhilaration and excitement most people feel on the downward free-fall from the top."

CHAPTER 34

End of the Journey

Getting up early the next morning after a sleepless night, we repacked the car, and after asking for suggestions for breakfast from the motel clerk when we checked out, we had a tasty breakfast at Lilo's Café. We travelled from Highway 66 back to Interstate 40, shortening our trip from Seligman to Las Vegas by about three hours. The timing would be perfect, as we should arrive at The Flamingo Hotel by early afternoon.

The closer we got to Las Vegas, the more butterflies I felt in my stomach. There was still a part of me that feared rejection again and who wanted to turn around, go back home, forget I ever discovered the skeleton in that drawer, and allow the secrets to remain hidden. I knew, however, that by abandoning my search now I would break Mama's heart and I would have to face the disappointment in myself that I would always feel. I knew I had no other choice but to face my greatest fear.

Finally, entering Las Vegas and turning onto The Strip, I was amazed by the vibrant and magical city, even though it was daytime. As we were driving to our hotel, we stared in amazement at the high-rise hotels, walking footbridges over four-lane intersections, casinos, restaurants, museums, shops, and thousands of people walking up and down the sidewalks. Following the map, which had been on my lap the entire trip, I directed K.C. to our destination.

Caesar's Entertainment re-built The Flamingo Hotel on the New Strip in 1946, and as Diane pointed out, has the distinction of being the oldest casino existing in the middle of the New Strip. I stared in awe at the bright pink building, with figures of flamingos behind a glass wall, framed by greenery pruned into flamingo shapes, and then looked up to see vivid pink flamingo wings fanned out with gold lights over the main entrance.

After handing our keys to the parking valet for Mama's convenience, we made our way into the lobby of this famous hotel, where I would finally meet the sister I had been searching for over the last twenty years.

When we walked into the hotel, the atmosphere was electrifying. The lobby had gleaming off-white floors, palm trees in various locations, and of course, pink flamingo signs and decals everywhere. The atmosphere was contagious, as tourists were scurrying around the lobby, lined with shops, restaurants, cafes, bars, and the casino. The sounds of the casino's whir of reels spinning, patrons dropping coins in slot machines, and the ensuing *cha-ching-a-ling* sounds, amid the cacophony of excited voices totally overwhelmed me. The scene playing out before me only added to the excitement and anticipation I was already feeling.

Since there was a long check-in line with guests just arriving, K.C. led Mama and me to the nearby Tropical Breeze Café and he returned to the lobby to wait in line and complete the check-in process. I ordered Mama and I each a glass of their specialty tea and we sat people-watching and listening to the musical sounds of the slot machines nearby.

K. C. finally returned, and said, "Our room is ready if you two are." I said, "I'm as ready as I'll ever be. Let's go!"

He led us to a row of gilded-door elevators, and we entered the first one available for our ride to the third floor. For Mama's sake, I had requested a suite on the lowest available floor so she would be more comfortable. As we entered our suite, the first thing which impressed me was the sheer size of the rooms; of course, I had never stayed in a hotel suite before. The floors were beautiful oak hardwood, the walls papered in pink, brown, and white silk wallpaper, pink accents scattered around, such as pillows on the plush sofa, the backs of the chairs in the dining area, and framed flamingo prints on the walls. Walking to the windows, I opened the curtains with a remote-control opener and gazed at the amazing scenes below and above me. As far as I could see, there were hotels, casinos, restaurants, gift shops, and museums to the left and right of our hotel. There were throngs of people walking up and down the sidewalks and crossing the elevated walkways over the boulevard to the same scene replicated on the other side.

After the bellhop delivered our luggage and pointed out all the amenities in the dining area and refrigerator, we started unpacking. Feeling as if I was coming back down to earth, I asked Mama and K.C., "Have either of you ever seen anything like this before?"

Shaking their heads, no, K.C. said, "Only on television!"

We had a chuckle at that, and after washing up and getting a cold drink out of the refrigerator, Mama said, "Margaret Ann, you're procrastinating. When are you going to call your sister?"

Knowing she was right, I said, "I was just getting ready to do that." Sitting down on the sofa, I picked up the magenta-colored room phone, dialed her number with shaking fingers, and listened impatiently as the phone continuously rang. Just as I was about to hang up, a female voice, which I recognized as Diane's, breathlessly answered, "Hello, Margaret, is it you? Are you finally here?"

With my voice quivering, I said, "Yes, Diane, I'm finally here."

I asked her if she wanted us to meet them downstairs in the lobby, but she said, "No, I think I would be more comfortable going up to your room, where we can have our first face-to-face meeting in privacy."

Agreeing with her, I gave her our room number and she said, "Well, I guess we'll finally be seeing each other for the first time in about an hour."

I responded, "I can't wait!"

Time seems to stand still when waiting on an important event to happen. I caught myself continuously looking at my watch and wondering if it had stopped running, because the hands never seemed to move. I wasn't aware I was pacing around the room until Mama, who was sitting on one of the dining room chairs, sewing on one of her baby blankets, said, "Baby, will you please stop that? You're driving me crazy!"

K.C., who was sitting at the other end of the table looked up from his crossword puzzle and said, "I agree with your Mama. Please sit down, take deep breaths, and try to relax."

I went to the refrigerator, found a Dr. Pepper, and sat down on the sofa. Even though I was physically still, however, my mind was racing. I wondered what these people, my blood relatives, would look like. *Would I see a resemblance?* After our first telephone conversation, Diane had mailed me pictures of herself, our mother, and other family members, but they were all taken years earlier. She told me she didn't have any recent pictures of herself because she disliked having her picture taken. When I first looked at them, I thought I saw a resemblance to Diane, but not so much to our birth mother,

As I sat on the sofa, looking out the window behind it, I noticed three people walking together, two men and a woman, as they entered the front door of our hotel. The woman was about my height, about my same weight, wore her blond hair in the same short style as mine, and shared the same way of carrying herself as I did. My friends always teased me about the way I walked, saying, "Margaret, you walk with a purpose, as if you're in a hurry to carry out a mission." I knew instantly the woman was Diane, and of course, Chummy must be the one holding her arm, and the other man must be Uncle Dennis.

I stood up and shouted, "They're here!"

Mama said, "Margaret Ann, you scared me to death! How do you know they're here?"

K.C. asked, "Are you sure?"

I replied, "I'm positive. I just saw three people walk into the hotel. I know the woman was Diane because she not only resembled me, but she walked and carried herself like me, and there were two men with her."

Taking a deep breath, I stood and waited. Mere minutes later, just as I thought, there was a light knock on the door. I froze, unable to respond.

Finally, K.C. asked, "Do you want me to answer it?"

Shaking my head, *no*, I made my way to the door and opened it.

CHAPTER 35

The Reunion

Standing just inches apart, we looked into each other's eyes, seeing the years of separation buried in their depths, and then hugged tightly, not wanting to let go in fear we might lose each other again. After shedding tears, we finally stepped back and stared at one another again. The reality of looking into her eyes, which were the same color as mine, was one of the most emotional moments of my life.

Composing ourselves, Diane and I finally laughed and realized we should let the others into the room and introduce our families to each other.

Mama, of course, was first in line to introduce herself to Diane, hugging her, and with tears running down her cheeks, said, "I didn't think I would ever live to see this day, Diane. You are still as beautiful as I remember you when you were just three years old.

K.C. stepped up, and said, "My turn," He then introduced himself by saying, "I can't tell you how happy I am to meet my sister-in-law," which brought tears to both of their eyes.

Diane introduced Chummy next, and with tears in his eyes, he gave me a bear hug, stepped back, and signed something to me. Diane translated, "Chummy said, 'You look so much like your sister, and I'm so happy to finally meet you.'"

I asked Diane, "How do you sign thank you?" She showed me, and as I signed those words to him, he chuckled, and we hugged again.

Uncle Dennis was last to introduce himself to me and gave me a warm hug. I backed up, looked into his blue eyes, and realized we also shared physical features. He was a very distinguished-looking man of medium height, slim build, with thick, curly white hair, a mustache, and sported a very dark suntan. With tears in his eyes, he said, "I am overjoyed to meet my sister's other daughter. Welcome to the family, Margaret." I found myself too choked up to answer him, but I nodded my head *yes* and hugged him again.

Looking around the room, I saw Mama still talking with Diane, as if they had always known one another, and I saw Uncle Dennis, K.C. and Chummy having no trouble communicating, as Chummy was able to read lips, K.C. was able to make up signs for different words or phrases that he could understand, and Uncle Dennis knew enough sign language to keep up with the conversation.

After everyone had finally finished hugging, crying, and talking, I composed myself and said, "To say I'm happy to meet all three of you is an understatement. Why don't we sit down while I get everyone something to drink?"

Opening the refrigerator door, I asked, "Would y'all prefer a soft drink, water, or coffee?"

They all chose a cold beverage and we sat down at the table. Chummy put his drink down and signed to Diane. She translated, "Chummy said 'I'm going to get the picture albums I left by the door when we walked in. Sis, these are the pictures of everyone on our mother's side of the family that I promised I would bring and share with you. We can go through them now or later, whenever you prefer.'"

While everyone else was talking and deciding to sit, Uncle Dennis walked up to me and said, "Margaret, I can't begin to tell you how much you remind me of my sister, not only in your physical characteristics, but in your mannerisms and speech pattern. I always thought there was no one who could talk as fast as Mayme, but after hearing you on the phone, and now in person, I think I've found her equal."

Laughing, I hugged him, and said, "Thanks, Unc. You have no idea what it means to hear you say those words."

He then continued, "Although I was younger than Mayme, I found myself taking on the role of big brother, always looking after her when she was in trouble, which was often," he heartily laughed again. I was fascinated by his laugh, which seemed to emanate from deep in his belly, and the jowls on each side of his face moved up and down with each "yuck."

Everyone was settling down, and the conversation turned to less emotional subjects, like our trip to Las Vegas, stories about Diane and Chummy's two sons and their families, and stories about Uncle Dennis and his family. He revealed he was divorced and had two daughters who lived in another state. Chummy did his share of contributing to the conversation, signing to Diane, who would then translate to us. He had a jovial personality and was constantly contributing funny stories.

Going to the refrigerator to get herself another drink, Diane asked, "Sis, are you ready to look through these albums?"

I said, "Absolutely, let's spread them out on the table."

Everyone moved in for a closer look as Diane started by saying, "Margaret, this album has copies of all the pictures I have in my family album at home. These are relatives on our mother's side of the family, including our grandmother's brothers and sisters, and even our great-grandmother and her family. I labeled each one so you will have background information on your ancestors and will be able to remember who they are when you look at them later."

I glanced up at her, again with tears in my eyes, and replied, "Diane, this is so sweet. I don't have words to describe how much this means to me. Thank you so much!"

Of course, this led to another hug and more tears from each of us. As Diane started going through the album page by page and giving brief stories about each picture, my head started spinning. After years of not knowing any blood relatives, seeing the faces and names of dozens of them all at the same time was overwhelming.

After we had looked through the entire album I got up and said, "I have something for you, too." Walking to my suitcase, I pulled out a picture album. Sitting down next to her, I said, "I made this for you. It's my life story in pictures, starting with the first picture of me right after Mama and Honey adopted me, through various grades in school, my graduation, my weddings, and other milestones in my life."

Diane, tearing up again, said "Aww, this is so sweet."

Looking through my memory album, Unc, Chummy, and Diane often remarked how I resembled Diane or Mayme when they were similar ages. The excitement of this new feeling of kinship and genetic connection was beyond anything I had ever experienced in my life. On the other hand, though, I couldn't help feeling guilty about how this may be affecting Mama, seeing my connection to this new family. I glanced at her, but she was smiling and seemed to be managing the situation well, enjoying all the old pictures and stories Diane told us about them.

After a couple of hours, Unc, chuckling, said, "I don't know about the rest of you, but I'm hungry enough to eat a horse. No offense intended towards you and your horses, K.C."

Laughing, we all agreed with him. K.C. said, "I hear there is a good buffet restaurant downstairs. Why don't we move this get-together to where the food is? My treat!" Of course, there were disagreements, but K.C. can be as stubborn as his parents when they insisted on us taking their car and extra money for the trip, and he wouldn't take no for an answer.

As we were walking out the room, Diane picked up the memory book I had given her and I said, "Sis, why don't you leave it here in the room, so you won't have to pack it around at the buffet? I'll bring it to you tomorrow."

Putting it back on the table, she said, "Good idea, Margaret, but don't you dare forget it!" Laughing at her ordering me around in a sisterly way, we linked arms and the six of us made our way down to the restaurant. After finishing a delicious meal, dessert, and coffee, we made plans for the next day.

Since we had agreed earlier that we would visit Mayme at her house, we decided it would be easier for all of us to meet there. Giving me our mother's address, along with directions, Diane said, "I think it will take us about the same length of time to get to her house as it will take you from here, so I'll call you in the morning when we're ready to leave. Our sons, Mark, and Kevin, are going to meet us there also, because they want to meet their new Aunt Margaret."

I said, "I can't wait to meet them, too, but I must confess, I'm scared to death at the prospect of meeting our mother."

Diane replied, "Don't worry, Margaret. I promise she won't have any idea who you are, so just pretend you're meeting a stranger."

Even if she had her mental faculties, she would still seem like a stranger to me, I thought, but said aloud, "Thanks for the reminder. I'll try my best to relax." We decided it was time for us to call it a night, so we hugged each other one more time and said our goodbyes.

The three of us took the elevator back up to our room, and as soon as we entered, I collapsed on the bed, feeling totally drained from today's experience and lack of sleep the night before.

K.C. said, "I know this reunion was an exhausting experience for you, but I felt it was rewarding and meaningful for everyone."

Looking at K.C. I said, "I agree, and I can truthfully say that I now have no regrets about the long and frustrating journey on which we have travelled to arrive at this day. The feeling of burying that skeleton tomorrow will finally give me closure.

Mama added, "Baby, I can't tell you how relieved I am right now. The reunion of you and Diane has been one of the biggest blessings of my life. I'm so happy for her as well, and relieved to see that she is genuinely happy in welcoming you into their family."

It was a tremendous relief to hear Mama's positive comments. The last thing I wanted was for her to feel hurt or jealous by my discovery. Thanking them both for their love and support through all the difficulties of the extended roller-coaster ride we had all been on, I gave them each a hug and kiss and made my way to the bathroom for a long, hot, soaking bath.

After my relaxing bath, I returned to the sitting area, opened the drapes, and sat speechless as I soaked in the true magic of Las Vegas, which a tourist can genuinely appreciate only only at night. Never in my life had I seen such an electrifying sight! Blinking neon lights of assorted colors lit every building. There were fountains in front of hotels spewing colored water high up into the air, other fountains were dancing, choreographed to music, and flashing billboards at the hotels advertised the names of the most famous entertainers in Hollywood who were appearing there. The animated faces of the throngs of tourists scurrying up and down the strip reflected the magical scene surrounding them. I called out to K.C. and Mama, "Y'all have to come over here and look at this!"

They walked over and shared the window with me, being equally as impressed as I was. After we pointed out various interesting things to one another, I glanced down at my watch and realized how late it was. Closing the curtains, I said, "Mama, you really need to go to bed. It's late, and this has been a long and emotionally exhausting day for you as well."

She said, "You're right, Baby, it has been, but mostly it's just been happy." She picked up her sewing basket, and I escorted her to the bedroom. K.C., who was already in the king-sized bed in the master bedroom, was working on a crossword puzzle, but stopped as I slid into bed and he said, "I'm so happy for you, Sweetheart. This has been a truly momentous day, but please try to get some sleep."

Knowing this would be a challenge, I said, "Thank you, my love. I'll try my best." After giving him a kiss, I turned off the light on my side of the bed, closed my eyes, and thought about the joys of the day. I couldn't stop focusing, however, on the most terrifying challenge I would face tomorrow, since discovering the skeleton in the drawer so many years ago. Saying a prayer for courage and peace and concentrating on deep breathing, I was finally able to fall into a fitful sleep.

CHAPTER 36

Shocking Conclusion

After tossing and turning, with nightmares of today's outcomes, I finally opened my eyes to see sunshine streaming through the cracks in the drapes. Even without turning over to see if K.C. was awake, I knew he was by the delicious aroma of fresh coffee wafting in from the kitchen area. Although we assumed the hotel would supply coffee in our suite, we decided to bring our own dark roast coffee from home. It turned out to be an excellent decision, as it seemed the further west we travelled, the weaker the coffee became. Stretching and pulling myself out of bed, I looked in on Mama and was happy to see she was still asleep. Seated at the table with his cup of coffee, K.C. was reading the newspaper the hotel had slid under our door. Leaning down to give him a kiss, I thanked him for brewing the pot of coffee.

He said, "You're welcome, my love. I know there's no need to ask how you slept last night. I'm very much aware from your restlessness, that it wasn't very peaceful."

I laughed and said, "You're one hundred percent correct, and I'm so sorry to have kept you awake as well."

Not surprisingly, he responded with his usual, "No problem!"

Pouring myself a cup of the black, steaming-hot liquid, I sat down at the table and leafed through the photo album Diane had given me last night. Pausing at a picture of our mother, I stared into the eyes of this woman who had given birth to me, and silently wondered if it were possible that she might have a memory of me when we met face-to-face. *Don't be foolish, Margaret,* I thought to myself. I remembered the telephone conversation I had with Diane the day I called to tell her we were coming, and her response.

She said, "Margaret, I'm so glad you will get the opportunity to see our mother before she dies, but I must warn you again that she will not be aware of who you are. Her dementia has progressed to the point where she frequently doesn't even recognize me or her husband, Bob. As soon as you told me you were coming, I started telling her, every time I went to their house, '*that baby*' is coming to see you soon, Mother, using the name you were referred to by our great-grandmother and grandmother, hoping that hearing the name they called you would somehow stir up memories. Sadly, Margaret, I never saw any reaction from her at all.'"

Mama interrupted my thoughts as she walked into the dining area and cheerfully said, "Good morning, you two! How did y'all sleep last night?"

Giving her a smile and a good-morning peck on the cheek I said, "Not very well, thank you! What about you?"

She said, "I'm sorry, Margaret, but I slept like a baby. The mattress on my bed is so comfortable I didn't want to get up this morning." Pouring herself a cup of coffee, she sat down next to me and looked at the picture of Mayme I had been studying. She said, "Baby, she is exactly as I remember her when we worked together so many years ago. I never told you before, but over the years I often thought about how you resembled her in so many ways."

Turning to look at her, I said, "That must have been very hard on you." She replied, "Yes and no. Mayme was a beautiful, vibrant woman and I was happy you shared some of those traits, but yes, I also felt a little sad and resentful because I wished so badly for you to have shared my genes instead."

I stood, walked over, and put my arms around the only mother I had ever known, and said, "I'm so sorry you had those regrets. The irony, Mama, is the fact that so many people have told me over the years how much I look like you."

She smiled and said, "I love you, Baby, and I'm so proud to have been the one who raised you."

K. C. interrupted by saying, "I'm sorry, but if you two want to get a bite to eat before it's time to meet your sister and some more family members, y'all need to get dressed and let's go."

We laughed and I said, "We're on our way!" Pouring myself a second cup of coffee, I told Mama she could have the bathroom first. I walked over to the window and looked down again upon the people teeming on the sidewalks, excitement clear on their faces as they scurried about, and the excitement seemed to radiate up to me as well.

Showering and dressing completed, Mama entered the living room and told me it was my turn. Entering the bathroom, I showered, looked at myself in the vanity mirror. and nervously fixed my hair and makeup. After do-overs I decided it didn't really matter how perfectly I looked because Mayme wouldn't know me with or without makeup. Finally calling myself presentable, I went into the living room and phoned Diane, to check on the time they expected to be at our mother's house.

She breathlessly answered the phone and said, "I'm sorry, Margaret, but we're running late because I've been trying to coordinate a time with my sons that will be convenient for each of them. The three of you have time to eat breakfast at the buffet if you all are hungry. When you've finished, call me and we will go from there."

I said, "That's fine, Diane. K.C. and Mama are hungry, but I think I have too many butterflies in my stomach to eat. We'll go downstairs anyway, and I'll call you when we get back up to the room."

After repeating Diane's message to K.C. and Mama, we went downstairs to eat at the breakfast buffet, since it would be quicker than table service at one of the specialty restaurants. I managed to nibble on a piece of toast and drank a glass of juice, while K.C. and Mama indulged in the wide variety of delicious breakfast offerings. After our meal, we went back up to our room to pick up Diane's album that I promised to bring to her and make the phone call to let her know we finished breakfast and were ready whenever she was.

She answered the phone and said, "Mark and Kevin have finally organized their day, and we're all ready to leave, so we'll meet at Mother's in thirty minutes or so. If you get there first, just wait in your car for us to arrive." I assured her I had no intention of entering our mother's house without her there for moral support.

We took the elevator down to the lobby, called for our car, and started on the scariest journey of my life. As we were riding down The Strip, following the directions Diane had given us, Mama said, "Margaret, I hope and pray Mayme is able to recognize you and me when we get there."

I said, "Mama, please don't build your hopes up. As I've told you before, Diane doesn't think there will be any chance of that happening because her dementia is getting worse by the day."

Sighing loudly, Mama said, "I can accept it if she doesn't recognize me, but I can always hope, and say a prayer, that she will somehow connect with you."

Turning around to look at her in the back seat, I said, "Mama, I don't want you to be disappointed. I promise I'll be okay if she doesn't recognize me. Please believe that."

Finally letting it drop, she started *oohing* and *aahing* at the various sights we were passing. Although the weather was very warm, the humidity was so much more tolerable than in our Southern climate. With my car window opened, I breathed in the healthy air of the Mojave Desert surrounding us, trying to calm myself down. Finally, leaving the hustle and bustle of the city, we travelled through valleys dominated with desert vegetation, with dry mountainous regions in the distance. After about thirty minutes, we arrived at the subdivision in which my mother and her husband lived.

The modest homes, mostly constructed of adobe, were situated amid a rocky landscape, with desert plants dotting the yards. As we pulled into the driveway of their house, we found Diane, Chummy, Uncle Dennis, and two nice-looking young men waiting for us. On the verge of hyperventilating, I sat in the car for a minute or two, taking deep breaths to calm me down.

Exiting the car, I walked over to Diane first and we exchanged a warm hug.

Turning to my nephews, I saw eyes looking at me that reminded me of the unusual color of my own, and I tearfully gave each of them a hug as Diane introduced them to us.

Of course, Chummy was standing there smiling at me and waiting his turn for a hug as well, signing, "I love you," which I now understood, and I signed it back to him. He laughed and hugged me tightly.

Unc was hanging back, and finally approached me with a hug and whispered, "Good luck, Margaret. I'm saying a prayer for you and for my sister. I know this must be a very emotional experience for you. Just remember, Mayme is suffering from dementia."

After Diane introduced everyone, we chatted among ourselves until we realized we were all getting uncomfortable from the heat of the midday desert sun beating down on the concrete driveway. Diane finally said, "Margaret, we'll be able to visit with each other again later, because we would like for you all to come to our house for dinner tonight. The boys will bring their wives, so you will also be able to meet them."

"That sounds wonderful, Diane. We appreciate it very much, and I cannot wait to meet the entire family."

Diane said, "Okay, I'm going to go in first to let them know everyone is here, to be sure Mother is physically prepared, and then I'll come back out and get the rest of you."

Diane finally stuck her head out of the door and said, "Come on in everybody, Mother and Bob are almost ready." Palms moist, with sweat dripping down my neck, I stepped inside the living room first, with the rest of the family following close behind. It took a while for my eyes to adjust to the lighting as I looked around the room. I then looked at Diane for instructions.

She said, "Margaret, why don't you and K.C. sit in these chairs," pointing to two chairs across from the couch, "because Mother usually likes to sit over there," as she pointed to a place on the middle cushion of the couch, and Bob usually sits next to her. Your Mama will be able to sit on the other couch cushion next to Mother. I'm hoping this seating arrangement will enable her to see you better, and I'm hoping the more she is able to look directly at you, the better the chance that she may recognize you. The boys, Chummy, and Unc, will hang out in the dining room, but will still be a part of our conversation, as it is an accessible area from there to the living room. I'm going to tell Mother and Bob their company is here and ready to meet them."

Minutes later, although it seemed more like hours, with my heart pounding so hard I felt as if everyone in the room could hear it, I looked up to see three people walking slowly down the hall from the back of the house into the living room. Naturally, my attention was on the woman in the middle of Diane and Bob. Mayme was slim built, a little taller than me, and was walking with an unsteady, but graceful stride as a handsome gray-haired man escorted her to the living room sofa. As he led her to the middle seat. she slowly sat down, back erect and feet crossed.

I couldn't help staring at her, all the while marveling at her meticulous and attractive appearance. She wore a long black-and-white paisley-printed skirt, an attractive long-sleeved white blouse with a deep V-neck, and she wore black low-heeled pumps. Besides rings on her fingers, the only other jewelry she wore was a pair of pearl stud earrings. Her reddish hair, obviously colored, was worn in a short and curly style. It was difficult to see the color of her eyes from where I was sitting, but they stared at me from behind a pair of large, red-framed glasses. Sitting regally on the sofa, she looked around, smiling, and nodding at everyone. Since I was sitting directly across from her, it was easy for us to have direct eye contact, but I saw no sign of recognition as she looked at me or anyone else in the room, including Chummy, Unc, Mark, and Kevin.

Finally, Diane pointed to me and said, "Mother, this is *that baby*."

Mayme turned to look where Diane was pointing, smiled, and nodded at me, but with no visible sign of recognition.

Mama, sitting beside Mayme on the couch cushion to the right of her said, "Mayme, remember me? My name is Lucy. We were friends and worked together years ago at the Markham Hotel in Gulfport."

She stared at Mama, but still only responded by smiling and nodding at her. Mama continued talking, telling her stories of fun times they had shared and people they worked with, but Mayme's response was always the same. I found myself sitting across from my birth mother and my adoptive mother, but I was at a total loss of words, not knowing what, if anything would be appropriate for me to say. My only contribution to the conversation was when either Diane or Bob asked me questions. To describe the situation as awkward would be a serious understatement.

Thankfully, Chummy had brewed a pot of coffee in the kitchen and Diane had brought a cake, so she said, "I think we would all enjoy some refreshments, so I'm going to cut the cake and Chummy and the boys will serve the coffee."

I got up and walked into the kitchen to help Diane serve the cake. As I handed the plate to Mayme, she looked up into my eyes and I held my breath, but she simply smiled and nodded once again. Thankfully, the conversation turned toward other subjects, such as our long road trip, Mark and Kevin's occupations and their children, stories by Unc, and K.C. adding stories of his horse business.

During this reprieve, however, I tried to keep up with the conversations around me, but the entire situation seemed so surreal I had trouble focusing on anything but my birth mother sitting across from me. Occasionally I would notice Mayme looking at me, but when I smiled or spoke to her, she only smiled and nodded back. After a couple of hours, it became obvious there would be no recognition on her part, and the visit was taking a physical toll on her and Bob.

Diane got up and I helped her pick up the dishes and clean the kitchen. When we re-entered the living room Diane said, "Mother, I think it's time for us to leave so you and Bob can get some rest."

Everyone stood up, hugs and handshakes with Mayme and Bob were exchanged between Diane and her family, as the three of us awkwardly made our way to the door. I lagged back, however, wanting one last opportunity to look at this woman who gave birth to me, because I knew I would never see her again.

As I turned and looked at her, I noticed she had taken a tentative step towards me. Mustering all the courage I had within me, I slowly walked toward her and extended my arms for a hug. Hesitating, she looked me deeply in the eyes, slowly opened her arms, and hugged me in return. Then the most powerfully emotional moment I had ever experienced in my life occurred. My birth mother whispered in my ear, "I love you." I stepped back, frozen, in total shock, and wasn't certain how to react or respond. Finally, with tears in my eyes, I approached her again for another hug, and whispered in her ear, "I forgive you."

She smiled, nodded, turned around, and walked back to her husband, who was waiting for her near the couch. She took Bob's arm and they slowly walked down the hall to their bedroom.

Taking what seemed forever to recover from such an overwhelmingly miraculous experience, I walked out of the house. All eyes were on me, as they could see that something profound had just occurred. I told everyone, in a trembling voice, what my birth mother had just said to me.

Diane and Mama burst into tears, and I could see tears in everyone else's eyes as well. After sharing more hugs, Diane said, "Margaret, Mother obviously recognized you on some level, because she has not rationally communicated with me or anyone else in a very long time."

The extremely emotional event affected everyone in the group and they each took turns hugging me, and of course followed by the shedding of more tears. Finally composing ourselves, the conversation turned to dinner tonight, with Diane giving us directions to their house and everyone promising to see each other later.

As we all walked to our vehicles, I looked back in the direction of the room which Mayme and Bob occupied, and I saw my birth mother in the window, smiling and nodding at me. This time, however, she added a little wave of farewell.

EPILOGUE

We stopped in Tucson on our way back to Louisiana and met my paternal nephew, Ryan. This fine young man impressed me, and I'm proud to be able to call him my nephew. He has now finished medical school, has a wife and three sons, and we continue to stay in touch with each other. I eventually met Ryan's father, my half-brother who called to welcome me to the family on Christmas Eve. We finally arranged a visit, and still stay in touch through phone calls and email.

Diane and I remain closely in touch by phone and email and try our best to visit each other in person every year or two.

My adoptive mother, so very thankful that I had finally found Diane, died peacefully in 2006.

Diane and Bob had my birth mother admitted into a specialized Alzheimer's care facility just a brief time after our visit and she died one year later.

Unc came to Louisiana to visit three times and we visited him at his home in Arizona. Sadly, he died in 2008.

My journey for self-identity, filled with the most extreme emotions one may experience, was not an easy one. Do I have regrets? Sure! I regret the aloofness I temporarily felt toward my wonderful adoptive family after discovering they were not my biological family. I regret not having the experience of growing up without my big sister. And I will forever be sorry for the pain I caused my paternal family by contacting them and bringing confusion and resentment into their lives.

Did I have an easier life than Diane's? Absolutely! Since my two loving parents raised me in a stable home, Diane, on the other hand, raised our mother and the experience of adjusting from one stepfather to another and moving from one town to another, deprived her of a stable home life.

I finally feel closure by solving the mystery of the skeleton I found in the drawer that day, but I will always wonder how my life and the lives of my birth parents might have been different had my father returned to Gulfport before my adoption.

If my readers can take only one thing from my story, I pray it is how and when to tell your child he or she is an adoptee. Please know it is never too early to start talking about the word "adoption," so it does not have a negative connotation when they get older and learn the truth. Start reading books to them about adoption, beginning when they are just babies. And most importantly, from an early age, let them know how special they are since you chose them to be your child.

ACKNOWLEDGMENTS

I would like to thank my family and friends who have shown me their unwavering love, support, and encouragement throughout this emotional journey. They have repeatedly read and re-read my manuscript, and still love me.

For my brilliant and supportive editing agent, Valerie Valentine, for taking a chance on a novice writer and offering much-needed ability and encouragement.

For a dear friend, Pam, who as an author herself, encouraged and coached me through my first attempts at getting my scrawlings to eventually read like a novel.

For Travis and Katie at Palmetto Publishing for steering me through the maze of steps involved in self-publishing my book.

For my Godson, Jason, special friends, Katlin, Randy, and Leesie for their help in guiding this computer-illiterate senior citizen through the myriad of technical computer issues I faced.

For my maternal sister, Diane, who encouraged me every step of the way in re-telling the story of the angst we felt and the challenges we faced in finding each other.

And for K.C., my soul mate, best friend, my love, my life, who emotionally supported me every step of the way.

CPSIA information can be obtained
at www.ICGtesting.com
Printed in the USA
BVHW091519220722
642785BV00012B/1198